LET ME BE
Your
TRUMPET

An Instrument in Your Hand

NANCY DENTON SANDERS

LET ME BE YOUR TRUMPET
AN INSTRUMENT IN YOUR HAND

Scripture taken from The Holy Bible, King James Version. Public Domain

iUniverse books may be ordered through booksellers or by contacting:

iUniverse
1663 Liberty Drive
Bloomington, IN 47403
www.iuniverse.com
844-349-9409

ISBN: 978-1-6632-2539-9 (sc)
ISBN: 978-1-6632-2540-5 (hc)
ISBN: 978-1-6632-2538-2 (e)

Library of Congress Control Number: 2021919803

Print information available on the last page.

iUniverse rev. date: 09/28/2021

O God How I Love Thee!

O God how I love thee,
Though Thy face not always I see,
At times I feel lonely and flounder,
Yearning only Your vessel to be.

A vessel now open and empty,
To be filled with love from Thee,
So full, free, and flowing to others,
That they may see.

Your loving kindness, Master,
Through a vessel such as me.

Nancy Denton Sanders
Scottsville, Virginia
1970

CONTENTS

DEDICATION

I dedicate this book to my beloved children: Dr. Timothy Andrews Crater, a compassionate physician, Laurie Crater Battles, a gifted writer, Leah Crater Lopez, a creative wife and mother, and Mary Crater Sharman, a passionate teacher of special education students.

They are the sunshine of my life. I get up every morning to pray for them. They have given me the honor of being called Mom, Mother, Mama, and one still calls me Mommy. God was so good to give me these four blessings. When they call me on the phone and I hear their voices, I smile inside and rejoice I am alive.

One of the best memories of their childhood was driving my station wagon with a car full of "little Crater faces." The noise of their chatter was beautiful family music. When they grew up and left home it was just too quiet. The silence was deafening.

I also dedicate this book to my beloved grandchildren: Reed Brooks Crater, Zoe Emerson Crater, Grace Warren Crater, Isabelle Holton Crater, Matthew Lee Battles, Jonathan

Denton Battles, Jackson Brooks Lopez, Nancy Kay Sharman, Joshua Thomas Sharman, and James Alexander Sharman.

The very thought of these boys and girls brings a smile to my face. I am so blessed that God gave these unique grandchildren to me.

PREFACE

When I was a young girl, I began to fast and pray when challenging situations would arise. I soon learned that the added blessing of these events was more than answered prayer, it was building intimacy with my Father God. It took a while for that to saturate my understanding. This is what God longs for from His children.

Just imagine if you only heard from your children on Sunday, and only a few words each day. It would not diminish your love for them. However, it would leave a vacuum in your heart. You would long to hear their voices. So, when we pray, we must listen and record what our Father has to say to us. It is wise instruction from the Author of the Universe.

I began to learn that time spent with God was so refreshing that I needed Him every day and many times during the day. As a result, I began my elementary approach of practicing the presence of God in everything I did during the day. His presence soon became so real, and I loved spending time with Him. Colossians 3:23 tells us "Do everything heartily as unto the LORD." No matter how small the job is, do it as if you were doing it for the LORD. It changes your attitude toward everything you do, even the things you do not like to do.

So, with these things in mind, I began to deepen my relationship with God. I must be honest and tell you that I have had many heart wrenching times in my life when I had to seek the Savior for my very life. I was heartbroken, broken in spirit, and crushed with these tragedies. One thing was always certain in my mind during these times. I knew my God would see me through victoriously, and He always did.

God is real and interested in our situations and circumstances. He longs to walk with us during our time of need. He also longs to hear from us when we simply want to spend time with Him. When we just want to praise Him and love Him in worship with singing, dancing, praying, and fasting.

Fasting is a powerful weapon in the arsenal of heaven. I quickly learned that I needed bread from heaven far more than I needed earthly bread. The mere discipline of denying the flesh to enrich and feed my spirit was far more rewarding.

I soon learned that time spent with God was so important that I could no longer survive the rigors of this life without spending time with Him in prayer and fasting. As a daughter of God, I cannot live without Him every day. He is my strength, my Father, and truly the lover of My soul.

I challenge you to begin this exciting journey with Him and know Him in a deeper dimension.

Joel 2:15: "Blow the trumpet in Zion, consecrate a fast, call a sacred assembly."

ACKNOWLEDGEMENTS

To my devoted husband, Bob, thank you for your love, support, patience, encouragement and especially for your prayers. You always appeared with a cup of coffee in your hand just when I needed one.

To my children, Tim, Laurie, Leah and Mary, who I am sure wondered "How much longer, Mom!" I appreciate your prayers and loving support.

To Dr. Emmanuel Chekwa for his enduring friendship over many years and for his encouragement as I wrote this book. He read many pages patiently. Thank you for your prayers.

To Laurie Battles, my daughter, for her enduring support, advice, patience and most of all for her linguistic skills. Without you, I would still be writing.

I thank God, my Father, for giving me the words and strength to make this book a reality. It is His book, and I am just His scribe.

CHAPTER 1
Introduction to Let Me Be Your Trumpet

We have all read dry, doctrinal treatises on how to become better Christians. This is not one. Try as we might, we have all endeavored, and, at one time or another, failed to enhance our spirituality by simply getting better at beating our flesh into submission as an act of our will. What if I told you that the key to rich, deep and lasting spiritual growth was found in a relationship? That's right. It is just that simple.

Many who have had a strained relationship with an earthly father have viewed our heavenly Father as a far away dictator who frowns on us from His heavenly throne as we feeble human beings try our best to perform for Him. Nothing could be farther from the truth. In the pages to come I have unveiled for you keys to an intimate relationship with the Creator of the Universe. The good news is that He eagerly awaits this intimacy with you. He has designed spiritual laws that provide for a close fellowship with Him. This means that you and He are literally one in Spirit. When we drop the quest to satisfy rules and regulations and, instead adopt a lifestyle of seeking to know Him personally, exciting things begin to happen! Our motives change and our lives are transformed.

Come along with me on an adventure through the living pages of God's Word, the Bible. We will watch miracles happen very often as God's people seek Him earnestly through fasting, prayer, waiting on Him and watching for Him as eagerly as a desert traveler seeks water. We will see God move over and over again as His saints seek, and as He has promised, to find Him again and again.

CHAPTER 2
The Power of Prayer and Fasting

Fasting is not a rowboat in the kingdom of God, it is a nuclear-powered submarine.

This is what fasting means to me: fasting is borne out of a deep longing for God, a depth of longing in my spirit that I have never experienced. A longing for my soul to be satisfied by the spirit of the living God. A longing to see His face and feel His warm embrace.

A longing for more of God and less of me. A longing that only His presence can bring. A longing to be filled fully with His presence. A longing to be filled that is so deep and so strong that He alone can fill the emptiness in my soul with His fullness. A longing that only His anointing can satisfy. A longing so deep that are no words in any language that can express it. Only words spoken in my prayer language will I ever be able to express my love for Him and, more importantly, what He has taught me.

A longing to be like His son Jesus, to show the world what God's loving kindness looks like. A longing to pray until the power falls! A longing to minister like the first century apostles. A longing that the great prophets of old had: Elijah, Isaiah, Ezekiel and men like David who was and is a "man after God's own heart." (1 Samuel 13:14). A longing to see His face and emanate His grace to a lost and dying world.

It is through the power of prayer and fasting that God can accomplish this through us. He can and He will if we do our part through prayer and fasting. The miracles of God will flow through us as they did the first century Christians. The gifts of the Holy Spirit will be activated as time is spent in His holy presence and they will flow through us like a mighty river.

Fasting is a spiritual warhead invading every facet of our lives. It is the beginning of intimacy with God, our holy Father. It is an expression of our great love for Him and His presence. It is the result of the desire of our hearts to know Him in a different dimension and it will empower us to live more victorious lives and go through life with an overwhelming love for Him—a love that is deeper than any we have ever known or felt before. This revealing knowledge of God will quicken the spirit of the living God and His ministry will be more powerful as His life flows more freely through us.

His face will shine upon us, and His love will emanate through us as we yield to Him more openly because we love Him more. As a result, we will open our hearts to be filled with a double portion of His love. We will be able to be a fountain of love flowing to a lost and dying world. God is calling His church to Himself. What an awesome invitation to come to the altar of the most-high God! It is an invitation we cannot ignore, for many are called, but few are chosen. Come to the altar to have your cup filled to the point of overflowing with God's love. Be so full of His glory that miracles will become a natural flow from the throne of God. These are His miracles; do not think that they are yours. You are simply a chosen vessel open to heal, deliver, and bring new life in Christ to those who do not know the love of God. They have been overwhelmed by a loveless religion that has rules that they know they cannot humanly keep. They have, understandably, given up.

God's love constrains and draws people to the altar. Once they know how much God loves them, they will come to love Him too.

We cannot impart His love until we know it. This is one of the most important facets of fasting—entering an intimate love relationship with God through the LORD Jesus Christ. We must fast to accomplish the work set before us. It is a goal from our Father God.

The earth is dry and in need of the river of God to replenish it. It is aching for the latter rain. Come and let's be a part of it, willing to do whatever it takes to minister through the full gospel. Yes, let's do all that God promised He would do through His people—humble people—who are willing to do His work and give *all the glory to Him.*

We must be willing to be an empty face for God to shine through. Willing for the world to see God through His

5

impartation from a faceless person. There is no claim to fame; we are simply an open vessel to be filled with God. That is the only face they need to see.

We can do nothing. He can do it all through us if we spend time in *prayer, fasting, listening* and *recording* His words. These words, that might have never been uttered before, will be spoken to us because they will flow from the Holy Ghost River that comes from the throne of the living God. Words of life—eternal life.

Oh! To be a conduit of God's love and grace to a lost and dying world. He can do it through us—God's children.

Let us go to our prayer closet, room, altar or wherever we can get alone with God and seek Him until the answers come. His words, straight from the throne room, are the only waters that will fill to overflowing the deep longing of our souls. This is the very fullness of God to finally complete our souls and fit us for kingdom service. Only through prayer and fasting can this be accomplished in us. Let us listen to His voice and spend time in His Holy Word to eat the literal *bread* of life. The Bible is the only living book in the whole earth. The only *living* book. It is God's breath of life and without *holy oxygen,* we will die. We will completely dry up.

God longs for His love to be made manifest through His people. We cannot achieve this; it is a gift from God borne out of hours spent with Him—hours of prayer, praise, and Bible study. Hours of listening to what He has to say to us and recording it to share with others. God gives us gifts that we may be able to gift others in the kingdom of God on earth.

In the fullness of time, if we seek His face, He will show us His face so indelibly that we will never forget it. And we will forever be changed. God is willing. Are we?

Oh! God, that we would be willing to do this so that we could become more like You! Then and only then will we have your peace to impart to others who are in the mire of sin. Their souls need the peace of God. They are empty. They only need to find out who and what they need to fill the God-shaped void down deep in their hearts.

Our fervent prayer should be: "Oh God, make me more like Jesus."

The Benefits of Fasting

- **Fasting helps subject our bodies to our spirit.**

  1 Corinthians 9:27: (Paul speaking) "But I discipline my body and bring it into subjection, lest, when I have preached to others, I myself, should be disqualified."

- **Fasting helps to discipline the body, mind, and spirit.**

  Proverbs 25:28: "Whoever has no rule over his own spirit is like a city, broken down, without walls.

This person knows no boundaries of his own and lets others invade his personal space, therefore, hindering his own spiritual growth as he tries to meet the needs of others.

- **Fasting subordinates our carnal desires to our spiritual desires.**

  Galatians 5:17: "For the flesh lusts against the Spirit, and the Spirit against the flesh; and these are contrary to one another, so that you do not do the things that you wish."

  The flesh is a growth inhibitor.

- **Fasting helps set the priorities in our lives.**

  Matthew 6:33: "But seek first the kingdom of God and His righteousness, and all these things shall be added to you."

  The kingdom of God should be our priority. God will take care of the rest.

- **Fasting is a longing for God.**

  Psalm 63:1-2: "O God, you are my God; early will I seek You; my soul thirsts for You; my flesh longs for You in a dry and thirsty land, where there is no water. So, I looked for You in the sanctuary to see Your power and Your glory."

David expresses a great longing for God. He was "a man after God's own heart." (1 Samuel 13:14 and Acts 13:22)

- **Fasting honors God.**

Luke 2:37: "And this woman was a widow of about eighty-four years, who did not depart from the temple, but served God with fastings and prayers night and day."

Anna was a precious prayer warrior who wanted to see the Messiah, God honored her prayer and she saw baby Jesus in the temple.

- **Fasting brings repentance for the Christian.**

James 4:8-10: "Draw near to God and He will draw near to you. Cleanse your hands, you sinners; and purify your hearts, you double-minded. Lament and mourn and weep! Let your laughter be turned to mourning and your joy to gloom. Humble yourselves in the sight of the LORD and He will lift you up."

Fasting cleanses and purifies our thinking. "You have turned my mourning into dancing; You have put off my sackcloth and clothed me with gladness" (Psalm 30:11).

He also promises to encourage us.

- **Fasting brings discernment.**

James. 5:13-15: "Is anyone among you suffering? Let him pray. Is any cheerful? Let him sing psalms. Is anyone among you sick? Let him call for the elders of the church, and let them pray over him, anointing him with oil in the name of the LORD. And the prayer of faith will save the sick, and the LORD will raise him up, and if he has committed sins, he will be forgiven."

Fasting makes us more sensitive to what God is calling us to do; therefore, it sharpens our discernment to the needs of others.

- **Fasting helps bring deliverance from sinful bondage.**

Isaiah 58:6-8:

"Is this not the fast that I have chosen: to loose the bonds of wickedness, to undo the heavy burdens, to let the oppressed go free, and that you break every yoke? Is it not to share your bread with the hungry, and that you bring to your house the poor who are cast out, when you see the naked, that you cover him, and not hide yourself from your own flesh? Then your light shall break forth like the morning, your healing shall spring forth speedily, and your righteousness shall go before you; the glory of the LORD shall be your rear guard."

Fasting also gives us boldness when we need to pray for the bondage of sin to be released from people who are struggling and want to be set free. He promises protection in that He is our rear guard.

- **Fasting helps destroy strongholds of doubt and unbelief.**

  Mark 9:29: "So He (Jesus) said to them, 'This kind can come out by nothing but prayer and fasting.'"

  Jesus encouraged fasting so we might be more effective in ministry.

- **Fasting increases confidence and effectiveness in prayer.**

  2 Corinthians 10:4: "For the weapons of our warfare are not carnal but mighty in God for pulling down strongholds."

  Spending time with God through prayer and fasting increases our faith, boldness and knowledge of how to pray against strongholds that keep God's people bound.

- **Fasting ushers in revelation.**

  This passage of scripture is an outstanding example of revelation knowledge, and it reveals how Daniel's fasts helped save these three young men.

11

Daniel 3:20-25:

And he (King Nebuchadnezzar) commanded certain mighty men of valor who were in his army to bind Shadrach, Meshach and Abed-Nego, and cast them into the burning fiery furnace. Then these men were bound in their coats, their trousers, their turbans, and their other garments, and were cast into the midst of the burning fiery furnace. Therefore, because the king's command was urgent, and the furnace exceeding hot, the flame of the fire killed those men who took up Shadrach, Meshach Abed-Nego. And these three men, Shadrach, Meshach and Abed-Nego, fell down bound into the midst of the burning fiery furnace. Then King Nebuchadnezzar was astonished; and he rose in haste and spoke, saying to his counselors, "Did we not cast three men bound into the midst of the fire?' They answered and said to the king, 'True, O king.' 'Look!' he answered 'I see four men loose, walking in the midst of the fire; and they are not hurt, and the form of the fourth is like the son of God.'"

God takes care of us during our trials and tribulations. He is a great Father, the best we could ever have.

- **Fasting may be a call to repentance.**

Joel 2:12-17:

"Now therefore,' says the LORD, 'Turn to me with all your heart, with fasting, with weeping, and with mourning. So rend your hearts, and not your garments; to return to the LORD your God for He is gracious and merciful, slow to anger and of great kindness; He relents from doing harm. Who knows if He will turn and relent, and leave a blessing behind Him—a grain offering and a drink offering, for the LORD your God? Blow the trumpet in Zion, consecrate a fast, call a sacred assembly; gather the people, sanctify the congregation, assemble the elders, gather the children and nursing babes; let the bridegroom go out from his chamber, and the bride from her dressing room. Let the priests, who minister to the LORD, weep between the porch and the altar, let them say, 'Spare your people, O LORD, and do not give Your heritage to reproach, that the nations should rule over them.'"

- **The land is refreshed.**

Joel 2:18-19: "Then the LORD will be zealous for His land and pity His people. The LORD will answer and say to His people, 'Behold, I will send you grain and new wine and oil, and you will be satisfied by them; I will no longer make you a reproach among the nations.'"

Corporate prayer and fasting are often neglected in churches and prayer groups. Some traditional churches neglect this responsibility and are weak because of it. They confuse politics with praying for the nation whose God is the LORD. Praying for the government to make godly decisions is not political; it is the act of humbling ourselves before God. He has promised that He will heal our land. This is established in 2 Chronicles 7:14: "If My people who are called by My name will humble themselves, and pray and seek My face, and turn from their wicked ways, then I will hear from heaven, and will forgive their sin and heal their land."

He promises to answer all our prayers. He will bring revival.

"O taste and see that the LORD is good" (Psalm 34:8).

Faith requires prayer and fasting for strength and growth. It helps Christians become more intimate with God. To fast means to abstain from physical food knowing that spiritual food is what your soul needs.

Fasting is one way to show God we are willing to be submissive to Him and His plan for us. In Psalm 35:13 David wrote: "But as for me, when they were sick, my clothing was sackcloth; I humbled myself with fasting; and my prayer would return to my own heart."

Fasting disciplines, the soul. In Psalm. 69:10, we read, "When I wept and chastened my soul with fasting, that became my reproach." Our whole focus becomes nourishing our spiritual man at this point.

The disciples asked the LORD why they could not heal the boy who was afflicted with epilepsy. Jesus said in Matthew 17:20–21: "Because of your unbelief, for assuredly, I say to you, if you have faith as a mustard seed, you will say to this mountain, 'Move from here to there,' and it will move; and nothing will be impossible for you. However, this kind does not go out except by prayer and fasting."

As we see in 1 Samuel 1:6-7 and 10, fasting manifests commitment before God. Hannah pressed into God so passionately in prayer and fasting that she laid hold of her miracle. In 1 Samuel: 1:6-7 we read "And her rival (Peninnah) also provoked her severely, to make her miserable, because the LORD had closed her womb. So, it was year by year, when she (Hannah) went up to the house of the LORD, that she (Peninnah) provoked her, therefore, she wept, and did not eat." And in 1 Samuel l:10 we read "And she was in bitterness of soul and prayed to the LORD and wept in anguish."

In Matthew 4:1-10, he tells us about Jesus being led into the wilderness to be tested by the devil. He had fasted forty days and forty nights, and he was hungry. Then Satan came to tempt Him. Jesus answered him with the living word of God after every temptation. Finally, Jesus said to him "Away with you Satan! For it is written, 'you shall worship the LORD your GOD, and Him only you shall serve'" Matthew 4:10).

Jesus was obedient to the Word of God. Fasting brings obedience. It is only to be seen by God. Remember how the Pharisees made a show of fasting? God did not think much of this. Fasting also strengthens the power of the Holy Spirit in the believer and gives us more victory over sin. It helps to maintain power over demons, develops faith, crucifies unbelief, and makes prayer more effective.

In Psalm 109:24 David wrote "My knees are weak through fasting, and my flesh is feeble from lack of fatness."

God called David a man after His own heart. I am sure that his prayer and fasting yielded an intimate relationship with his Father God. David also showed earnestness and complete faithfulness in his devotional life. He wrote many psalms of praise to his Father. All believers who are seeking God would find fasting a great spiritual experience that grows their faith and brings them closer to the heart of God. No regulations or set rules are given as to how long or how often. That is determined by individual desire and needs.

The following passages emphasize this fact: Matthew 9:14-15, 1 Corinthians 7:5 and Acts 13:1-5. However, Acts 13:2-3 is the best example of this concept: "As they ministered to the LORD and fasted, the Holy Spirit said, 'Now separate to Me Barnabas and Saul for the work to which I have called them.' Then, having fasted and prayed, and laid hands on them, they sent them away."

When God says something three times it is established.

Scriptures that support the biblical **principle of fasting:**

Luke 10:19: Jesus said: "Behold, I give unto you authority to trample on serpents and scorpions, and over all the power of the enemy, and nothing shall by any means hurt you."

Psalm 91:13: "You shall tread upon the lion and the cobra, the young lion and the serpent you shall trample underfoot."

David fasted often and this verse affirms the fact that it brings great strength when it is needed.

Psalm 69:10: "When I wept and chastened my soul with fasting, that became my reproach."

David was fasting due to overwhelming troubles, which almost swallowed him.

Psalm 69:14-15: "Deliver me out of the mire and let me not sink; let me be delivered from those who hate me, and out of the deep waters. Let not the floodwaters overflow me, nor let the deep swallow me up; and let not the pit shut its mouth on me."

Psalm 69:17-20 "And do not hide your face from your servant, for I am in trouble; hear me speedily. Draw near to my soul and redeem it; deliver me because of my enemies. You know my reproach, my shame, and my dishonor; my adversaries are all before You. Reproach has broken my heart, and I am full of heaviness; I looked for someone to take pity, but there was none; and for comforters, but I found none."

This psalm ends with David praising God: "I will praise the name of God with a song and will magnify Him with thanksgiving" (Psalm 69:30). "The humble shall see this and be glad; and you who seek God, your hearts shall live" (Psalm 69:32). "Let heaven and earth praise Him, the seas and everything that moves in them" (Psalm 69:34).

This is an example of the fact that fasting assures submission before God to the exclusion of all else. Moses, Joshua, Elijah, and Jesus were the only ones who are recorded as having fasted forty days.

The duration of a fast may be forty days or as brief as a portion of a single day, as in Israel's case in 2 Samuel 1:11-12.

God seekers whose historic fasts are recorded the Bible:

Who Fasted	Duration	Bible Reference
Ahab		1 Kings 21:27-29
Judah		2 Chronicles 20:1-25
Judah		Ezra 8:21-23
Ezra		Ezra 10:6-17
Nineveh		Jonah 3:5-10
Nehemiah		Nehemiah 1:4
Jews		Esther 4:16
David		Psalm 35:13, 69:10,109:24
John the Baptist's Disciples		Matthew 9:14-15
Anna		Luke 2:36-38
Hannah		1 Samuel 1:1-7
Church at Antioch		Acts 13:1-3
Paul		Acts 27:9-11

Who Fasted	Duration	Bible Reference
Cornelius		Acts 10:30-31
Many Churches		Acts 14:23
Paul		2 Corinthians 6:5, 11:27
David	One day	2 Samuel 3:35
Judah	One day	Nehemiah 9:1-4
Judah	One day	Jeremiah 36:6
Daniel	One day	Daniel 9:3, 20-27
Pharisees	One day	Luke 18:9-14
Israel	One day	Judges 20:26-35
Israel	One day	1 Samuel 7:5-15
David	One day	2 Samuel 1:12
Darius	One night	Daniel 6:18-24
Esther, Mordecai	Three days	Esther 4:16
Many People	Three days	Matthew 15:32
Paul	Three days	Acts 9:9
David	Seven days	2 Samuel 12:16-18
Israel	Seven days	1 Samuel 31:13
Paul and 276 Men	Fourteen days	Acts 27:33
Daniel	Twenty-one days	Daniel 10:3
Moses	Forty days	Deuteronomy 9:9-11; 10:10
Joshua	Forty days	Exodus 24:13-18
Elijah	Forty days	1 Kings 19:8
Jesus	Forty Days	Matthew 4:1-11

God seekers who prayed and fasted:

Ahab
1 Kings 21:17-26, 27-29

1 Kings 21: 17-26

The word of the LORD came to Elijah, the Tishite, saying, "Arise, go down to meet Ahab king of Israel, who lives in Samaria. There he is, in the vineyard of Naboth, where he has gone down to take possession of it. You shall speak to him, saying 'Thus says the LORD: "Have you murdered and taken possession?"' And you shall speak to him, saying, 'Thus says the LORD "In the place where dogs licked the blood of Naboth, dogs shall lick your blood, even yours."' So, Ahab said to Elijah, 'Have you found me, O my enemy?' and he answered, 'I have found you, because you have sold yourself to do evil in the sight of the LORD: behold, I will bring calamity on you. I will take away your posterity and will cut off from Ahab every male in Israel, both bond and free. I will make your house like the house of Jeroboam the son of Nebat, and like the house of Baasha, the son of Ahijah, because of the provocation with which you have provoked Me to anger and made Israel sin.' And concerning Jezebel the LORD also spoke, saying, 'The dogs shall eat Jezebel by the wall of Jezreel. The dogs shall eat whoever belongs to Ahab and dies in the city, and the birds of the air shall eat whoever dies in the field."' But there was no one like Ahab who sold himself to do wickedness in the sight of the LORD, because Jezebel his wife stirred him up. And he behaved very abominably in following idols, according to all that the Amorites had done, whom the LORD had cast out before the children of Israel.

Now, 1 Kings 27-29 we see Ahab fasting and humbling himself before God:

So it was, when Ahab heard those words, that he tore his clothes and put sackcloth on his body, and fasted and lay in sackcloth, and went about mourning. And the word of the LORD come to Elijah the Tishbite, saying, 'See how Ahab has humbled himself before Me? Because he has humbled himself before Me, I will not bring the calamity in his days. In the days of his son I will bring the calamity on his house."

Judah
2 Chronicles 20:1-5

2 Chronicles 20:1-5

"It happened after this that the people of Moab with the people of Ammon, and others with them besides the Ammonites, came to battle Jehoshaphat.

Then some came and told Jehoshaphat, saying, 'A great multitude is coming against you from beyond the sea, from Syria; and they are in Hazazon Tamar' (which is in En Gedi). And Jehoshaphat feared, and set himself to seek the LORD, and proclaimed a fast throughout all of Judah. So Judah gathered together to ask help from the LORD; and from all the cities of Judah they came to seek the LORD. Then

Jehoshaphat stood in the assembly of Judah and Jerusalem, in the house of the LORD, before the new court."

Jehoshaphat's prayer: 2 Chronicles 20:6-12:

O LORD, God of our fathers, are you not God in heaven, and do you not rule over the kingdoms of the nations, and in Your hand is *there not* power and might, so that no one is able to withstand you? Are you not our God, who drove out the inhabitants of this land before Your people Israel, and gave it to the descendants of Abraham Your friend forever? And they dwell in it and have built You a sanctuary in it for Your name, saying, if disaster comes upon us—sword, judgment, pestilence or famine—we will stand before this temple and in Your presence (for Your name is in this temple), and cry out to you in our affliction, and You will hear and save. And now, here are the people of Ammon, Moab, and Mount Seir—whom you would not let Israel invade when they came from the land of Egypt, but they turned from them and they did not destroy them—here they are, rewarding us by coming to throw us out of Your possession which You have given us to inherit. O, Our God, will you not judge them? For we have no power against this great multitude that is coming against us; nor do we know what to do, but our eyes are upon You.

2 Chronicles 20:13:22

Now all Judah, with their little ones, and their wives, and their children, stood before the LORD. Then the Spirit of the

LORD came upon Jahaziel, the son of Zecharaiah, the son of Benaiah, the son of Jeiel, the son of Mattaniah, a Levite of the sons of Asaph in the midst of the assembly. And he said, 'Listen, all you of Judah and you inhabitants of Jerusalem, and you, King Jehoshaphat! Thus says the LORD to you. *'Do not be afraid nor dismayed; because of this great multitude, for the battle is not yours, but God's.* Tomorrow go down against them, they will surely come up by the Ascent of Ziz, and you will find them at the end of the brook before the Wilderness of Jeruel. *You will not need to fight in this battle.* Position yourselves, stand still and see the salvation of the LORD, who is with you, O Judah and Jerusalem! Do not fear or be dismayed; tomorrow go out against them, for the LORD is with you.' And Jehoshaphat bowed his head with his face to the ground and all Judah and the inhabitants of Jerusalem bowed before the LORD worshipping the LORD. Then the Levites of the children of the Kohathites and of the children of the Korahites stood up to praise the LORD God of Israel with voices loud and high. So, they rose early the next morning and went out into the Wilderness of Tekoa; and as they went out, Jehoshaphat stood and said, 'Hear me, O Judah and you inhabitants of Jerusalem: Believe in the LORD your God and you shall be established; believe His prophets, and you shall prosper.' And when he had consulted with the people, he appointed those who should sing to the LORD, and who should praise the beauty of holiness, as they went out before the army and were saying: 'Praise the LORD, For His mercy endures forever.' Now when they began to sing and to praise, the LORD set ambushes against the people of Ammon, Moab, and Mount Seir, who had come against

23

Judah; and they were defeated. (An angelic host may have been the force that set about the ambushes.) For the people of Ammon and Moab stood up against the inhabitants of Mount Seir to utterly kill and destroy them. And when they had made an end of the inhabitants of Seir, they helped to destroy one another.

The troops turned on each other. A spirit of confusion descended upon them, and they became very disoriented. The result was they killed themselves and nobody won that battle. This is the same miraculous happening that will take place at the battle of Armageddon where, no doubt, angels will be present and resurrected saints will also be there to fight this final battle.

2 Chronicles 20:24-25:

"So, when Judah came to a place overlooking the wilderness, they looked toward the multitude; and there were their dead bodies, fallen on the earth. No one had escaped. When Jehoshaphat and his people came to take away their spoil, they found among them an abundance of valuables on the dead bodies and precious jewelry, which they stripped off for themselves, more than they could carry away; and they were three days gathering the spoil because there was so much."

In 2 Chronicles 20:29-30 we read: "And the fear of God was on all the kingdoms of those countries when they heard that the LORD had fought against the enemies of Israel. Then the realm of Jehoshaphat was quiet, for his God gave him rest all around."

This miraculous defeat became known by all nations surrounding Judah. Not in all history, up to this time, had there been such a defeat on earth. This battle was unique as it combined earthly soldiers led by God and His angels. It took "three days to gather all the spoil because there was so much" (2 Chronicles 20:25).

Jehoshaphat's powerful prayer before Judah and Jerusalem was very long. Listed below are the powerful petitions and affirmations that he raised to God.

1. You are the God of our Fathers.
2. You are the God of Heaven.
3. You have all power and might.
4. None can understand You.
5. You rule over all the kingdoms of the heathen.
6. You are our God.
7. You drove the Canaanites before Israel.
8. You gave Your land to the seed of Abraham.
9. You have dwelled there.
10. They have built You a sanctuary for Your name.
11. You will hear and answer us when we cry in our affliction.
12. Now the Ammonites, Moabites, and the Edomites are come to conquer us.
13. Will you not judge them?

14. We have no might against such a company.
15. We do not know what to do.
16. Our eyes are upon You.

Solomon's special plea for help is much like Jehoshaphat's.

It is found in 2 Chronicles 6:28-31: "When there is famine in the land, pestilence or blight or mildew, locusts or grasshoppers; when their enemies besiege them in the land of their cities; whatever plague or whatever sickness there is; whatever prayer, whatever supplication is made by anyone, or by all Your people Israel, when each one knows his own burden and his own grief, and spreads out his hands to this temple: then hear from heaven, Your dwelling place, and forgive, and give to everyone according to all his ways, whose heart You know (for You alone know the hearts of the sons of men), that they may fear You, to walk in Your ways as long as they live in the land which You gave to our fathers." (This is just a portion of his prayer.)

Judah
Ezra 8:21-23

Daniel and Ezra were both Babylonian Jews and their books bear a resemblance. Ezra was president of the great synagogue and wrote this book. He also helped settle the canon of Jewish scripture. They wrote about fasting and prayer for protection.

Ezra 8:21-23:

"Then I proclaimed a fast there, at the river of Ahava, that we might humble ourselves before our God, to seek from Him a right way for us, and our little ones, and all our possessions. For I was ashamed to request of the king an escort of soldiers and horseman to help us against the enemy on the road: because we had spoken to the king, saying, 'The hand of our God is upon all those for good that seek Him, but His power and His wrath are against all of them that forsake Him.' So we fasted and entreated our God for this and he answered our prayer."

Ezra 8:31-32:

"Then we departed from the river of Ahava on the twelfth day of the first month, to go to Jerusalem. And the hand of our God was upon us, and He delivered us from the hand of the enemy, and from ambush along the road. So, we came to Jerusalem, and stayed three days."

Ezra
Ezra 10:6,14,17

Ezra continued fasting and praying for Israel.

Ezra continued fasting and praying for Israel. In Ezra 10:6 the Bible tells us: "Then Ezra rose up from the house of God and went into the chamber of Jehohanan son of Eliashib; and when he came there, he ate no bread and drank no water, for he mourned because of the guilt of those from the captivity."

Ezra called them all of Israel together. He told them if they did not come in three days, they would be denied food. Then all the men of Judah and Benjamin gathered in Jerusalem for three days and all the people sat in the street of the house of God trembling because of this matter.

Ezra then preached a sermon demanding separation from strange wives. The Israelite men had taken heathen women as their wives. These women did not worship the LORD God Almighty. They worshiped pagan gods and Ezra was upset.

Ezra's sermon was very direct as he told the whole assembly in Ezra 10:14 "Please, let the leaders of our entire assembly stand; and let all those in our cities who have taken pagan wives come at appointed times, together with the elders and judges of their cities, until the fierce wrath of our God is turned away from us in this matter." He continued in Ezra 10:17: "By the first day of the first month they finished questioning all the men who had taken pagan wives."

Ezra was a great man of God and an outstanding administrator. God had laid this matter on his heart, and he gave it all he had. God gave the victory. They made an end to this matter. It was settled!

Nineveh
Jonah 1:1-2,15, 3:2, 5-10

We see Jonah's first commission by God in Jonah 1:1-2: "Now the word of the LORD came to Jonah the son of Amittai, saying, 'Arise go to Nineveh, that great city, and cry out against it; for their wickedness has come up before Me.'"

Jonah immediately found a ship headed for Tarshish, boarded it, went down into the lowest parts of the ship and fell fast asleep. This did not last long as the ship sailed into treacherous seas and everyone on board was afraid. They were so afraid they began to throw cargo off the ship. Finally, the captain of the ship found Jonah and asked him to pray to his God "so that we may not perish." The mariners cast lots to find out why this trouble had come upon them, and the lot fell to Jonah. They asked him many questions and he said: "I am a Hebrew; and I fear the LORD, the God of heaven, who made the sea and the dry land" (Jonah 1:9).

Jonah was honest, telling the people on board that he was the reason for the terrible sea. He told them that they should pick him up and throw him into the sea. However, the men continued to row hard, trying to return to land, but they could not. In Jonah 1:15: we learn that "they picked up Jonah and threw him into the sea, and the sea ceased from its raging." Soon thereafter the great fish that the LORD had prepared swallowed Jonah, and he was in the belly of the fish three days and three nights.

Jonah came out of the belly of the whale a different man. The LORD spoke to him a second time and he was obedient. In Jonah 3:2 we find his second commission with the LORD saying to him, "Arise, go to Nineveh, that great city, and preach to it the message that I tell you."

In Jonah 3:5-10 the Bible tells us:

"So the people of Nineveh believed God, and proclaimed a fast, and put on sackcloth, from the greatest of them to the least of them. Then word came to the king of Nineveh; and he arose from his throne and laid aside his robe, covered himself with sackcloth and sat in ashes. And he caused it to be proclaimed and published throughout Nineveh by the decree of the king and his nobles, saying, Let neither man nor beast, herd nor flock, taste anything; do not let them eat or drink water. But, let man and beast be covered with sackcloth, and cry mightily to God; yes, let everyone turn from his evil way from the violence that is in his hands. Who can tell if God will turn, and relent, and turn away from His fierce anger, that we may not perish?' Then God saw their works, and that they turned from their evil way; and God relented from the disaster that He had said He would bring upon them, and He did not do it."

Fasting and prayer were once again mighty weapons of warfare against Satan. God's word prevailed and saved Nineveh because of their humility before Him and their perseverance in prayer and fasting.

Nehemiah
Book of Nehemiah

Nehemiah was a very talented man. He was chosen by God for a great undertaking which was insurmountable in scope and sequence. On every page of the thirteen chapters in Nehemiah there was a man with a mission to restore the wall of Jerusalem and bring the Jews back to serving their God. He was indeed a great restorer of the ruins in Jerusalem and the spiritual needs of Israel. Nehemiah was an excellent leader who had good communication skills, was a positive motivator, an articulate administrator, and a gifted problem solver. Additionally, he had a servants heart to please God.

He demonstrated the very embodiment of the central theme of this book: abandonment of self in a whole-hearted pursuit of God's will.

It is important to note before we begin the story of Nehemiah, the visionary builder, that chapters one through seven report the restoration of the wall and the problems that arose from the enemies of the Jews. They were in much need of protection.

In chapters eight through ten Nehemiah deals with the people inside the walls. God reveals to him that they are in spiritual need of restoration. They had been living in Babylon and had not been worshipping God. They needed to remember the Book of the Law of Moses and repent. Ezra read the law to them, they repented and sealed the covenant.

In chapters eleven through thirteen we find the names of the people recorded who lived in Jerusalem and the reestablishment of Israel. The wall was formally dedicated. The temple order and worship were restored. During this period Nehemiah returned to Jerusalem after twelve years. He found that several situations needed to be rectified.

In the last verse of Nehemiah he prayed, "Remember me, O my God, for good" (Nehemiah 13:21)! He was the ultimate prayer warrior.

The story unfolds

The first chapter takes place in Shushan (now called Susa), the ancient winter capital of the kings of Persia, in the month of December 446 BC Nehemiah was cupbearer to King Artaxerxes and a trusted friend. This was a very important position and a well-respected one as he had to taste the wine before the king drank it. This insured that it was not poison and would not kill the monarch. He lived in the palace and was well paid as only a person of impeccable character was allowed to be that close to the king.

Sad word came to Nehemiah from his brother Hanani and a few friends from Judah. When Nehemiah asked, "How are the Jews who have survived the captivity and how is Jerusalem?" In Nehemiah 1:3 we read "And they said to me, 'The survivors who were left from the captivity in the province are in great distress and reproach. The wall of Jerusalem is also broken down and its gates are burned with fire.'" When he heard these words, he wept and mourned. He sat down fasted and prayed before the "God of heaven." Nehemiah addressed his Father as the "God of heaven" many times.

It became time for him to take wine to the king. He was very sad, and the king had never seen him sad. He asked Nehemiah "Why are you so sad I have never seen you like this before." He told the king of the bad news he had been given and the king immediately asked him what he needed. Nehemiah then prayed to the God of heaven before answering the king. "And I said to the king, 'if it pleases the king would you send me to Judah, the city of my fathers' tombs, that I may rebuild it" (Nehemiah 2:5). The king gave him permission to go, and Nehemiah asked for letters to the governors of the region beyond the river so they would permit him to pass through on his way to Judah. He also asked the king for a letter to Asaph the keeper of the king's forest. He needed timber to rebuild the gates of the wall near the temple, city wall and a house for him. The king granted his request.

The king even sent armed captains and horseman with him on this journey. So, Nehemiah took the letter written by the king to the governors of the region and they granted him permission to pass through their region. Once again, God had made a way. This was a journey that lasted twelve years and changed history.

Nehemiah arrived in Jerusalem and went in the night with a few men to view the walls. "I told no one what God had put in my heart to do" (Nehemiah 2:12). Now it was time for him to tell the Jews, the priests, the nobles, the officials, and the others who would do the work. He shared with them what God had put in his heart. He wanted to rebuild the wall and the gates so that Jerusalem would no longer be a reproach. He included the words of encouragement from his king. In Nehemiah 2:18 the Bible says, "So they said, 'Let us rise up and build.' Then they set their hands to this good work.

Then the wicked triumvirate arose; Sanballat, Tobiah and Geshem. They were disturbed that a man had checked on the children of Israel. These enemies laughed and ridiculed the workmen on the wall and jeered them with questions. Nehemiah did not answer their questions. He simply affirmed God's sovereignty and reminded them that they had no heritage, nor civic or religious rights in Jerusalem. Without saying it he meant to convey that they should mind their own business because he was directing God's business and God's work.

Nehemiah was a wonderful communicator and further told them that the God of heaven would help them build the wall and restore the great city.

This crowd appears again so let us realize just who they were. Sanballat was a Horonite, Tobiah was an Ammonnite and Geshem was an Arab, most likely from the region south of Judah. Many years after Israel had first possessed the Promised Land there were old enemies who wanted to keep Jerusalem in ruins. These men were probably among them.

Also, in Nehemiah 6:14 we find Nehemiah praying, "My God, remember Tobiah and Sanballat, according to these their works, and the prophetess Noadiah and the rest of the prophets who would have made me afraid." This was a very effective prayer against his enemies. Nehemiah was powerful and persistent in prayer. He also recognized the fear these minions were trying to instill in the men of God who were doing His work. The love of God rules over any fear that comes our way if we pray and believe.

In chapter three we see the great administrator who is organizing the groups of workers and assigning them their specific tasks in rebuilding the wall. There were thirty-two groups assigned to special areas. The groups were named, and work began on their assignments. Nehemiah showed great leadership in this magnificent plan to finish this task in an orderly fashion.

The rebuilding began with Eliashib, the high priest and his priests, who built the Sheep Gate. They consecrated it and then hung the doors, then continued building to the Tower of the Hundred and consecrated it. Their final task was to the Tower of Hananel. There were thirty more groups given detailed assignments like those given to Eliashib and his men. The last assignment was between the upper room and the corner as far as the Sheep Gate. The goldsmiths and the merchants made these repairs.

Two interesting events occurred while the wall was built. Shallum and his daughters made repairs. It was very unusual for women to do construction work at this time in history. It is also noted in chapter three verse five that when the Tekoites made repairs their nobles did not work. This seems to indicate a passive resistance against Nehemiah's leadership. It was just another stumbling block to God's work.

When Nehemiah listed the groups he often wrote after each group "next to them" or "after them" showing the continuity of the project. There were groups who made repairs indicating inspection of the work. He was the consummate administrator. Every detail was checked so that when the wall was finished it was a strong completed wall.

Nehemiah accepted his assignment from God seriously and always wanted to do his best. He often prayed to the God of heaven saying "Remember me, O my God concerning this"(Nehemiah 13:14). He had the heart of a servant.

In chapter four the wall is defended from enemies and their ridicule continues. The evil triumvirate returns. Sanballet became angry when he heard that the wall was being restored and the mocking began. He spoke to his brother and ranted, "What are these feeble Jews doing? Will they fortify themselves? Will they offer sacrifices? Will they complete it in a day? Will they revive the stones from the heap of rubbish— stones that are burned" (Nehemiah 4:2)? Then Tobiah joined in the ridicule, "Whatever they build, if even a fox goes up on it, he will break down their stone wall" (Nehemiah 4:3).

Nehemiah prayed a powerful prayer asking God for judgment on the enemies of His plan. The workmen resumed the work and the wall restored to half the original height. This interference of the mockers gave the people a stronger motivation to work.

Once again news spread that the wall was being restored and the gaps were coming together. Again, Sanballat, Tobiah, the Arabs, the Ammonites, and the Ashdodites became angry. The enemies began to grow in number. They conspired to attack Jerusalem and create confusion. (The devil showed up.)

Nehemiah always approached God in prayer when people tried to hinder His work. The people prayed and kept on working. A watch was set day and night.

Judah reported to Nehemiah that the workers were failing and that there was so much rubbish they were not able to build the wall. He continued that the adversaries said, "They will neither know nor see anything, till we come into their midst and kill them and cause the work to cease" (Nehemiah 4:11). The Jews who lived near the wall were hearing evil threats repeatedly and became very fearful. This approach was designed to upset them, and they cried to Nehemiah about the growing problem. The wicked ones were feeling threatened by the success of the builders and increased their fear mongering.

Nehemiah tightened the security and gave swords, spears, and bows to the families. He spoke to the nobles, leaders, and the rest of the people saying "Do not be afraid of them. Remember the LORD, great and awesome and fight for your brethren, your sons, your daughters, your wives, and your houses" (Nehemiah 4:14).

This message to the people working on the wall gave them such great devotion that they worked beyond sunset. It encouraged them to stay God-focused! They worked on the construction with one hand and held a weapon with the other.

At times the workmen felt isolated so Nehemiah appointed a trumpeter who was by his side, and he instructed all workers on the wall that if they had a problem the trumpeter would sound the alarm, and everyone was to gather with him. He reminded them, "Our God will fight for us" (Nehemiah 4:20).

He then told the people that each man and his servant would stay in Jerusalem at night to guard. The builders worked night and day. In Nehemiah 4:23 we read, "So neither I, my brethren, my servants, nor the men of the guard who followed me took off our clothes, except that everyone took them off for washing."

They were battle-prepared!

In chapter five Nehemiah deals with oppression. Prior to Nehemiah's arrival in Jerusalem, a famine and a need to pay taxes had forced many families into great financial need. These poor people began to cry out for justice for they had found a champion in Nehemiah. He was angry about these circumstances and began to help them. "I also, with my brethren and my servants am lending them money and grain. Please stop this usury" (Nehemiah 5:10).

He called a meeting of the nobles and the rulers and asked them why they were subjecting the people to such harsh usury. They were charging them interest on their lands, vineyards, olive groves, and their houses. They were also charging them a hundredth of the money made on the grain, the new wine and the oil.

Nehemiah told them to restore their lands, vineyards, olive groves as they had foreclosed on them. They were gouging the people with interest. He told them it has to stop now! He continued that they must also forgive their claims on the money grain, new wine and olive oil. They immediately said, "We will restore it and require nothing in return; we will do as you say" (Nehemiah 5:12).

He called the priest and required an oath from them vowing that they would keep this promise. Nehemiah then stood and shook out the fold of his garment and said, 'So may God shake out each man from his house and his property, who does not perform this promise. He will be shaken out and emptied.' And all the assembly said, 'Amen!' and praised the LORD. Then the people did according to this promise (Nehemiah 5:13).

Nehemiah was a very honest man. The twelve years he had been governor neither he nor his brothers used the governor's provision. Former governors had put burdens on the people as they took bread and wine and forty shekels of silver. Even their servants ruled the people. He feared God and his servants did not treat the people in that manner. They continued to work on the wall, and they did not buy land. His servants came to work. They worked for the people without charge.

Nehemiah was a kind and generous man. At his table he fed one hundred Jews, and rulers as well as those who came to him from the nations. In Nehemiah 5:18-19, we read, "Now that which was prepared daily was one ox and six choice sheep. Also, fowl was prepared for me, and once every ten days an abundance of all kinds of wine. Yet despite this, I did not demand the governor's provisions, because the bondage was heavy on this people. "Remember me, my God, for good, according to all that I have done for this people."

After dealing with the oppression of the people Nehemiah's next challenge was a conspiracy to assassinate him. In chapter six the evil triumvirate once again appeared. Sanballat, Tobiah and Geshem had heard there were no breaks in the wall. They sent a letter to Nehemiah inviting him to meet them in the plain of Ono. He knew they meant to harm him, so he sent a message to tell them he was doing a great work. Why should he leave and go down to see them? They sent this letter four more times and he sent his same letter back.

Finally, Sanballat sent his servant with a threatening letter. In this letter he said that the Jews were planning to rebel and according to these rumors Nehemiah was rebuilding the wall so that he could become their king. Sanballat threatened to report these findings to the king. Nehemiah answered the letter saying, "No such things as you say are being done, but you invent them in your own heart" (Nehemiah 6:8).

Nehemiah recognized the plot was designed to make them afraid. In doing so they would not be strong enough to finish the wall. He then prayed asking God to strengthen their hands.

These enemies were relentless. They were not through. Nehemiah went to the house of Shemaiah and Shemaiah suggested they meet in the house of God and close the doors of the temple. He told Nehemiah that his enemies were going to kill him, and it would probably be in the night.

Nehemiah realized it was another plot and refused to go to the temple. He knew that Tobiah and Sanballat had hired Shemaiah to do this. If he had accepted this plot and gone into the temple, they would have given an evil report and ruined his reputation. They would have lied about Nehemiah meeting in the temple as they were his enemies.

He then prayed against his enemies saying, "My God, remember Tobiah and Sanballat, according to their works and the prophetess Nodiah and the rest of the prophets who would have made me afraid" (Nehemiah 6:14).

The wall was completely restored in fifty-two days. The people rejoiced! All the surrounding nations were sad. They feared Nehemiah and the Jews. "And it happened when all our enemies heard of it, and all the nations around us saw these things, that they were very disheartened in their own eyes; they perceived that this work was done by our God" (Nehemiah 6:16).

In Nehemiah 6:17-18 we learn that Tobiah and his son had married women from prominent families in Jerusalem. These relatives appeared to be part of a spy network against Nehemiah and spread rumors within Jerusalem. They also gave support to the fear-mongering letters in order to frighten him. Many nobles of Judah sent letters to Tobiah and Tobiah sent many letters to them. Evil often operates in high places.

In chapter seven the wall had been built, the doors had been hung, and the gatekeepers, singers and the Levites had been appointed. Nehemiah also appointed his brother Hanani as governor of Jerusalem and Hananiah as head of security. Nehemiah's authority was absolute as he was governor of Judah and he reported to the king.

At this time the city was large with few people in it as the houses were not rebuilt. God directed him to gather the nobles, rulers, and the people so they could be registered by genealogy. It was at this time he found a register of those Jews who came up in the first return from Babylonian captivity. This list is written in verses six through seventy-two. We read in verse seventy-three "So the priests, the Levites the gatekeepers, the singers, some of the people, the Nethinim, and all Israel dwelled in their cities" (Nehemiah 7:73). The priests, Levites, security guards, singers, Temple's assistants and other people lived in Jerusalem. The rest of the Israelites found a place to live in their own towns.

In chapters eight through ten the Jews were encouraged to return to their covenant and worship. They gathered in front of the Water Gate to hear Ezra read the Book of the Law of Moses to them. They had prepared a wooden platform for him to stand on so all the people could see him. The Jews had lost most of the knowledge of the Torah because of their captivity in Babylon.

When Ezra the scribe opened the book and prayed all the people stood up and worshiped the LORD. Everyone wept when they heard the law being read by Ezra. They were repenting and happy to be returning to God. The Levites and others helped them to understand the law. "And Nehemiah who was the governor, Ezra, the priest and scribe, and the Levites who taught the people said to all the people, 'This day is holy to the LORD your God; do not mourn nor weep.' For all the people wept, when they heard the words of the Law. Then he said to them, 'Go your way, eat the fat, drink the sweet, and send portions to those for whom nothing is prepared; for this day is holy to our LORD. Do not sorrow for the joy of the LORD is your strength'" (Nehemiah 8:9-10).

What a great celebration! They were rejoicing because they had repented and been forgiven.

Now on the second day of the revival Ezra began to teach them the understanding of the Book of Law, and the Feast of the Tabernacles was restored. They continued to study the Torah and dedicate themselves to understanding it. The feast lasted seven days. On the eighth day there was a sacred assembly.

In chapter nine the children of Israel fasted in sackcloth with dust on their heads. The Israelites separated themselves from all foreigners and confessed their sin and the iniquities of their fathers. They stood for the reading of the law for one-fourth of the day. For another fourth of the day they confessed and worshiped the LORD. "And the Levites, Jeshua, Kadmiel, Bani, Hashabniah, Sherebiah, Hodijah, Shebaniah," and Pethahiah, said: 'Stand up and bless the LORD your God forever and ever! Blessed be Your glorious name, which is exalted above all blessing and praise'" (Nehemiah 9:5)!

They had to relearn the Torah and dedicate themselves to the instruction given to them by God's word through Moses.

Nehemiah 9:38 says, "And because of all this, we make a sure covenant and write it; our leaders, our Levites, and our priests seal it."

In chapter ten of Nehemiah we read that the Israelites entered a covenant with God. The people who placed their seal on the covenant were listed with Nehemiah being the first name on the list. All their names are recorded in verses one through twenty-seven. The contents of the sealed covenant were explained in verses twenty-eight through thirty-nine. There were customs acquired in Babylon that needed to be addressed. These areas of concern were mixed marriages, honoring the Sabbath, being committed to offerings, tithes, and proper care of the temple. In verse twenty-eight it seems that practically everyone followed their leaders in a solemn oath to keep the Law. The Israelites were committed to keeping the covenant.

In chapters eleven through thirteen the people were restored to God's word. The wall was dedicated, and the temple worship was restored. Nehemiah returned for a visit and instigated reforms.

Nehemiah was challenged with designing a repopulation program. The leaders lived in Jerusalem. The rest of the people cast lots and one out of ten would live in the holy city while nine-tenths were to live in other cities.

Nehemiah's administrative skills were once again noted as this plan was peacefully accepted by the people. His great talent exhibited in his organization and communication skills resulted in a smooth transition. The plan was carefully executed with success.

Chapter twelve includes lists of priests and Levites from the original return under Zerubbabel until the time of Nehemiah.

Nehemiah dedicated the wall.

The Levites came from all places to Jerusalem bringing their instruments of cymbals, psalteries, and harps. They came with gladness, thanksgiving, and singing. "Also that day they offered great sacrifices, and rejoiced, for God had made them rejoice with great joy; the women and the children also rejoiced, so that the joy of Jerusalem was heard afar off" (Nehemiah 12:43).

This was a loud celebration!!

Later Nehemiah established the temple order and worship. He appointed leaders with detailed instructions. Everyone knew their responsibilities.

In the final chapter of Nehemiah, the people read from the Book of Moses and learned that no Ammonite or Moabite should ever come into the congregation of God for they had not graciously welcomed the children of Israel with bread and water. They had even hired Balaam to put a curse on them. However, their God turned it into a great blessing. As a result of this treatment, they separated all the mixed multitude from Israel. The Israelites instituted principles of separation. This was done to insure that never again would the remnant turn aside to add other gods to their worship of God.

The reforms of Nehemiah

Eliashib the priest, had authority over the storerooms in the temple and he allied himself with Tobiah, who was one of the evil triumvirate. The priest prepared a large room for Tobiah in the temple. Prior to this everything in that room was to be given to the Levites, singers, and gatekeepers. The offerings for the priests were also housed there. This storeroom was filled with grain offerings, frankincense, worship vessels and tithes of grain, new wine and oil.

Nehemiah had returned to the king. Later he asked for permission to leave. He went back to Jerusalem and discovered all the evil that Eliashib and Tobiah had done. They had prepared a room for Tobiah in the courts of the house of God. Nehemiah was so angry that he threw all Tobiah's household goods out of the room. He demanded that all the room be cleansed, and he brought back the frankincense, the worship vessels, and the grains. The storeroom was restored.

Then he found that the Levites had not been given their food portions. As a result, the Levites and the singers had gone back to their farms. Nehemiah contended with the rulers and asked, "Why is the house of God forsaken" (Nehemiah 13:11). He gathered all of them together and admonished them sharply. All Judah brought the tithe of the grain, and the new wine and the oil to the storehouse. This completely replenished what had been taken from this special room in the temple.

The Israelites were given jobs and instructions as to how they should be done. Nehemiah also appointed staff members who were honest men to make sure that the appointees were doing their jobs correctly. These were honest men who were responsible for distributing to their brothers.

Nehemiah prayed "Remember me, O my God, concerning this, and do not wipe out my good deeds that I have done for the house of my God, and for its services" (Nehemiah 13:14).

The next reform was about keeping the Sabbath holy. Nehemiah saw people treading wine presses and loading donkeys with grapes, figs and all kinds of burdens that they brought to Jerusalem on the Sabbath day. He contended with the nobles again, saying to them, "What evil thing is this that you do, by which you profane the Sabbath day" (Nehemiah 13:17)?

He then commanded that the gates of Jerusalem be shut as it began to get dark the day before the Sabbath and charged the gatekeepers they would not be opened until after the Sabbath day. The merchants and the sellers camped outside the gates once or twice. Nehemiah warned them that if they came again, he would use force to drive them away. They did not come again on the Sabbath. He also commanded the Levites to cleanse themselves and guard the gates on the Sabbath day.

Nehemiah prayed saying: "'Remember me, O my God concerning this also, and spare me according to the greatness of Your mercy'" (Nehemiah 13:22)!

The next challenge was when he saw Jews who had married women from pagan nations. They were from Ashdod, Ammon, and Moab. I contended with these men, told them what I thought about their actions, even slapped some of them and jerked them by the hair. Nehemiah also "made them swear by God, saying 'You shall not give your daughters as wives to their sons, nor take their daughters for your sons, or yourselves'" (13:25). He continued to admonish them about how King Solomon had married pagan wives and that it caused him to sin. "And one of the sons of Joiada, son of

Eliashib the high priest, was a son-in-law of Sanballat, the Horonite; therefore, I drove him from me" (Nehemiah 3:28).

In the final words of the Book of Nehemiah he prayed, "Remember me, O my God, for good" (Nehemiah 13:31).

God chose Nehemiah to be the savior of the Israelite nation. He had prepared him for this very moment in Jewish history. When Nehemiah was very young, He was grooming him for this great appointment in his life. He was one of His chosen to restore the Israelite nation to Himself. Twice Nehemiah said "It was put in my heart" when speaking of rebuilding his beloved Jerusalem. He not only restored the walls, he restored the Jews to their Father God. He will always be remembered as being the restorer of physical and spiritual Israel.

He had the heart of a servant. This was proven when he left his prestigious job of cupbearer to King Artaxerxes I. The cupbearer also had to be a very brave individual as he was at risk of his own death. He left the palace where he lived leisurely to rebuild the wall in Jerusalem. The holy city lay in ruins.

Nehemiah became a trusted servant and close confidant of the king. So, when he heard that Jerusalem, the city of his father's tombs lay in ruins. he was very sad. No one was ever to be sad before the king. It was a well-understood unspoken rule and one that was not to be broken without consequence.

As Nehemiah served the king one day, he asked him why he was so sad. He shared his heartbroken story. The king understood him and asked what he could do to help. Nehemiah prayed to the God in Heaven and then he told the king what he needed. The king was more than generous and allowed him to go to Jerusalem. He also sent building materials and wrote letters to the governors of countries that he would need to travel through to arrive safely in Jerusalem. He also sent military people with Nehemiah on the trip to the holy city.

Nehemiah gladly received this with much gratitude and happiness of heart. The builder of the wall was on his way to begin the mission that God had called him to so long ago. His Father had prepared him for this moment in time.

Nehemiah had a heart to serve and an eye to see what had to be done. It was an overwhelming job if not seen through God's eyes. Nehemiah also had an ear to hear the voice of God. He prayed to his Father before every task and took on every problem that arose during construction. The enemies of the Jews rejoiced in the ruins of Jerusalem. They were upset when Nehemiah began to restore the wall and the gates that had been burned.

Nehemiah was a prayer warrior and because of this he could clearly hear the voice of God. This intimacy with God gave him great encouragement to see the wall standing in his mind's eye when it yet lay in ruins. He kept this focus throughout the trials of building the wall. By faith he was able to see the finished product. The wall was one-and-a half miles long and it was completed in fifty-two days. The nations all around were afraid. They realized that the God of Israel had completed it. The thought of a powerful God showing His favor to Israel put great fear in their hearts.

Once the wall was completed Nehemiah turned his heart to spiritually restoring the Jews to their religious heritage. He asked Ezra, the priest, to come and read the Book of the Law of Moses to them. They worshipped and prayed to God. They began to realize how living in Babylon had infected their faith. After crying, repenting, and asking God for forgiveness, they felt renewed.

This was the beginning of restoration of their faith in God. They wrote a covenant that contained all the changes that needed to be made in their hearts and minds. It was sealed. They promised to keep the covenant and restored the Feast of the Tabernacles.

Nehemiah then began to set the temple in order. This surely pleased the heart of God. In these acts of restoring Israel back to God, we see him as the spiritual savior of Israel. They had come from Babylon, a pagan nation, to the holy city where they began going to the temple, honoring God, and living by the Torah. It was a great revival that God had planned so long ago when he chose Nehemiah, his trusted servant, to complete this wall and bring a spiritual renewal. Only our God could do these extraordinary works.

To Him be all honor and glory.

Jews
Esther 4:1-3,13,16; 7:1-10; 9:13-14; 10

The book of Esther is a story of a beautiful, young Jewish girl who becomes Queen of Persia. Her husband was King Ahasuerus, who reigned from 486-465 B.C. Esther was a vessel chosen by God to save the Jewish people who lived in one-hundred-twenty-seven provinces over which her husband ruled. Abihail was Esther's father. Mordecai was her uncle, who had adopted her as a daughter. Queen Esther was not only a godly woman, but she was also a very brave woman who trusted God.

Haman, who was an enemy of the Jews, was promoted by the king to be above all the princes who were with him. Therefore, all the king's servants were to bow before Haman. Mordecai refused to bow. Haman was livid about this disrespect and devised a plan to destroy all the Jews throughout the whole kingdom of Ahasuerus.

This was another one of Satan's attempts to destroy the very people of God through whom the Messiah, the Savior of the world would come. So, Haman approached the king that a decree be written to destroy all the Jews who lived in the kingdom of Ashasuerus. He asked for four reasons.

The first reason was that the Jews were different from all other people.

The second reason was that they did not keep the king's laws. Their behavior upset Haman.

The third reason was that they did not profit the king; therefore, the king had a financial concern.

The fourth reason was "to bring it (silver) into the king's treasuries" (Esther 3:9).

Haman offered to pay ten thousand talents of silver into the king's treasuries to get rid of them at $1,920 for each Jew. The silver would probably be added to the king's silver chest with this program. (Sounds like a lucrative business deal.) This decree was to be sent to one-hundred-twenty-seven provinces, from India to Ethiopia. All were under the reign of King Ahasuerus.

The king called the scribes to write the degree and have it delivered to all provinces over which her husband ruled. This copy of the document was issued into law and published to all the people. It was a cruel document that would annihilate all the Jews—men, women, and children—in one day. The document also stated that all their possessions would be plundered. This cruel deed was to be executed on the thirteenth day of the twelfth month, which is the month of Adar.

The king took off his signet ring and gave it to Haman. This was a sign that Haman had the king's full royal authority over this plan. A letter of annihilation was sent to all the king's provinces, and there was great mourning among the Jews. Mordecai did what most godly men would do in times of trouble: he fasted and prayed. He walked the streets in sackcloth wailing, and he came to the king's gate even though no man was allowed to do so in sackcloth. The Jews were surprised and responded with great mourning, fasting in desperation, weeping and wailing.

In Esther 4:1-3 we read: "When Mordecai learned all that had happened, he tore his clothes and put on sackcloth and ashes and went out into the midst of the city. He cried out with a loud and bitter cry. He went as far as the front of the king's gate, for no one might enter the king's gate clothed with sackcloth. And in every province where the king's command and decree arrived, there was great mourning among the Jews, with fasting, weeping, and wailing; and many lay in sackcloth and ashes."

Mordecai sent a message to Esther that he wanted her to go to the king on behalf of the Jewish people. She told him that she had not been summoned to the king's quarters for thirty days. Mordecai replied, "Do not think in your heart that you will escape in the king's palace any more than all the other Jews" (Esther 4:13).

After considering all these happenings, Esther told Mordecai in Esther 4:16: "Go, gather all the Jews who are present in Shushan, and fast for me; neither eat nor drink for three days, night or day. My maids and I will fast likewise. And so, I will go to the king, which is against the law; and if I perish, I perish!"

In chapter five Esther went to the king and he extended the golden scepter to her. She asked the king to have a banquet and invite Haman. Haman was excited and went to the banquet.

After the banquet the king did not sleep well, and he called for the book of the records; and they were read to him. In these records it was found that Mordecai had told of Bigthana and Teresh, two of the king's eunuchs, who sought to kill the king. The king immediately wanted to honor Mordecai and asked who was in the court. It was Haman. So, he asked him, "What shall be done for the man whom the king delights to honor" (Esther 6:6)? Haman eagerly laid out very lavish plans for this event. So, the king called Mordecai to tell him of the honor that he was giving him. Haman had laid out plans for Mordecai thinking he was the one to be honored. Things were beginning to look dim for Haman.

Esther 7:1-10

"So the king and Haman went to dine with Queen Esther. And on the second day, at the banquet of wine, the king again said to Esther, 'What is your petition, Queen Esther? It shall be granted you. And what is your request, up to half the kingdom? It shall be done!' Then Queen Esther answered and said, 'If I have found favor in your sight, O king, and if it pleases the king, let my life be given me at my petition, and my people at my request. For we have been sold, my people and I, to be destroyed, to be killed, and to be annihilated. Had we been sold as male and female slaves, I would have held my tongue, although the enemy could never compensate for the king's loss.' So King Ahasuerus answered and said to Queen Esther, 'Who is he, and where is he, who would dare presume in his heart to do such a thing?' And Esther said, 'The adversary and enemy is this wicked Haman!' So, Haman was terrified before the king and queen. Then the king arose in his wrath from the banquet of wine and went into the palace garden; but Haman stood before Queen Esther, pleading for his life, for he saw that evil was as determined against him by the king. When the king returned from the palace garden to the place of the banquet of wine, Haman had fallen across the couch where Esther was. Then the king said, 'Will he also assault the queen while I am in the house?' As word left the king's mouth, they covered Haman's face. Now Harbonah, one of the eunuchs, said to the king, 'Look! The gallows, fifty cubits high, which Haman made for Mordecai, who spoke good on the king's behalf, is standing at the house of Haman. Then the king said, 'Hang him on it.'" So, they hanged Haman on the gallows.' Then the king's wrath subsided."

In Esther 9:13-14, we read, "Then Esther said, 'If it pleases the king, let it be granted to the Jews who are in Shushan to do again tomorrow according to today's decree, and let Haman's ten sons be hanged on the gallows.' So the king commanded this to be done; the decree was issued in Shushan, and they hanged Haman's ten sons."

We see victory for Mordecai in Esther 10:3: "For Mordecai the Jew was second to King Ahasuerus and was great among the Jews and well received by the multitude of his brethren, seeking the good of his people and speaking peace to all his country men."

What story of *victory* for God's people! The favor of God abundantly abounded on Esther and Mordecai as they fasted and prayed to save the Jewish people living under the rule of King Ahasuerus. He reigned over a vast territory, from India to Ethiopia.

All glory, honor, and praise to Almighty God for His wondrous works!

David
Psalm 35:13, 69:10, 109:24

Psalm 35:13: "But as for me, when they were sick, my clothing was sackcloth; I humbled myself with fasting; and my prayer would return to my own heart."

Psalm 69:10: "When I wept and chastened my soul with fasting, that became my reproach."

Psalm 109:24: "My knees are weak through fasting, and my flesh is feeble from lack of fatness."

David was a great man of God who had an intimate relationship with his heavenly Father. Fasting is a very effective way to nestle close to the Great God of Heaven who is also our Abba Father. It shows great dedication and involves time well spent on our knees.

John The Baptist's Disciples
Matthew 9:14-15

Matthew 9:14-15: "Then the disciples of John came to Him, saying, 'Why do we and the Pharisees fast often, but Your disciples do not fast?' and Jesus said to them, 'Can the friends of the bridegroom mourn as long as the bridegroom is with them? But the days will come, when the bridegroom shall be taken away from them, and then they will fast.'"

Anna
Luke 2:36-38

Luke 2:36-38:

"Now there was one, Anna, a prophetess, the daughter of Phanuel, of the tribe of Asher. She was of a great age and had lived with a husband seven years from her virginity; and this woman was a widow of about eighty-four years, who did not depart from the temple, but served God with fastings and prayers night and day. And coming in that instant she gave thanks to the LORD, and spoke of Him to all those who looked for redemption in Jerusalem."

Just who was Anna? She is mentioned in the Bible as a prophetess and one of the people associated with baby Jesus. She was the daughter of Phanuel from the tribe of Asher. Her name, which she shared with Hannah in the Old Testament, means "favor" or "grace." All we know about her is found in three verses in the New Testament book of Luke. Three very powerful verses. When Anna encounters the infant Jesus in the temple, we see that her life is indeed overflowing with favor and grace. She is among only a few women in the Bible who bear the title "Prophetess." The others are Miriam, the sister of Moses (Exodus15:20), Deborah, the judge (Judges 4:4),

Huldah the wife of Shallum (2 Chronicles 34:22), Isaiah's wife (Isaiah 8:3) and Philip's four unmarried daughters (Acts 21:8-9). Many translations indicate that Anna was eighty-four years old when she met Jesus; however, it is also possible to translate the text to mean that Anna lived eight-four years after her husband died. If Anna married at fourteen years old, lived seven years with her husband, then eighty-four years after his death she would have been one-hundred- and-five-years old when she held her Savior in the temple.

It is believed that Anna was given living quarters in the temple because of her designation as a prophetess, and the fact that the Levite singers lived in chambers in the temple. What is noteworthy about Anna is her deep devotion to prayer and fasting for many years of her life. The desire of her heart was granted with an encounter with her Savior. It was worth it all when she beheld the Messiah, the one she had long awaited.

Mary and Joseph arrived at the temple with the baby Jesus to satisfy the Old Testament Law. They needed to make the purification offering (Leviticus 12:6-8) and to present Jesus as their firstborn before God. (First born consecration was mandated in Exodus 13:2.) While they were there a man named Simeon cradled the LORD Jesus in his arms, praised God and uttered a prophecy concerning Jesus and Mary. At this moment, Anna entered the temple, immediately recognized Jesus as the long-awaited Savior and began thanking God. Luke tells us that "she spoke of Him to all who looked for the redemption in Jerusalem" (Luke 2:38).

Anna was one of the first to bring honor to baby Jesus and one of the first to share the good news of His birth. It was meant to be shared, and Anna shared it with everyone who was anticipating the Messiah. The redeemer had come, the prophecies were being fulfilled, and Anna was blessed to witness this historic event in the temple.

She was a devout woman of great faith in her God, and her life was marked by prayer and fasting.

Hannah
1 Samuel 1:7, 1 Samuel 4:4, Psalm 22:3

1 Samuel 1:7 "So it was, year by year, when she (Hannah) went up to the house of the Lord, that she, (Peninnah, Elkanah's other wife who had given Elkanah sons and daughters), provoked her; therefore, she wept, and did not eat."

Hannah knew the place of prayer. She went to the tabernacle, which was God's house. It was there she fasted and prayed for a child. Hannah went there because that was where the presence of Almighty God remained. David recognized this in Psalm 22:3 as he wrote "But You are holy, enthroned in the praises of Israel."

This emphasizes the fact the LORD dwells in the praises of His people.

Samuel, the great prophet of old, also recognized this fact in I Samuel 4:4: "So the people sent to Shiloh, that they might

60

bring from there the ark of the covenant of the LORD of hosts, who dwells between the cherubim."

God also dwells in the praises of His people in the New Testament. He is an awesome God worthy of all praise. Hannah recognized this fact and lived a life marked by prayer and fasting for a breakthrough. She was granted a son as a result.

The Church at Antioch
Acts 13:1-3

Acts 13:1-3: "Now in the church that was at Antioch there were certain prophets and teachers: Barnabas, Simeon who was called Niger, Lucius of Cyrene, Manaen who had been brought up with Herod the tetrarch, and Saul. As they ministered to the LORD, and fasted, the Holy Spirit said, 'Separate to Me Barnabas and Saul for the work to which I have called them.' Then, having fasted and prayed, and laid hands on them, they sent them away."

Revealed in this chapter is that early Christian leaders fasted and prayed before sending apostles out to minister the gospel of Jesus Christ.

Paul
Acts 27:9-11, 27:33

"Now when much time had been spent, and sailing was now dangerous because the Fast was already over, Paul advised them, saying, 'Men, I perceive that this voyage will end with disaster and much loss, not only of the cargo and ship, but also our lives.' Nevertheless, the centurion was more persuaded by the helmsman and the owner of the ship than by the things spoken by Paul" (Acts 27:9-11).

Acts 27:33: "And as day was about to dawn, Paul implored them all to take food, saying, 'Today is the fourteenth day you have waited and continued without food, and eaten nothing.'"

Paul and the men aboard the ship had fasted, prayed, and God answered their prayers.

Cornelius
Acts 10:30-33

Cornelius and his and the members of his household were the first gentiles to hear the gospel since Pentecost.

Acts 10:30-33: "So Cornelius said: 'Four days ago I was fasting until this hour; and at the ninth hour I prayed in my house, and behold, a man stood before me in bright clothing, and said, 'Cornelius, your prayer has been heard, and your alms are remembered in the sight of God. Send therefore to Joppa and call Simon here, whose surname is Peter. He is lodging in the house of Simon, a tanner, by the sea. When he comes, he will speak to you.' So I sent to you immediately, and you have done well to come. Now therefore, we are all present before God, to hear all the things commanded you by God.'"

Peter preached a *powerful sermon* to Cornelius' household, including relatives and close friends. Here are the main points of Peter's sermon.

Here are the main points of Peter's sermon.

- Salvation comes by faith.
- God is no respecter of persons.
- The word of God provides for bodily healing for all.
- Christ is judge of the living and the dead.
- Remission of sin through Jesus Christ for *all* who believe.

(Read the whole chapter with emphasis on verses 30-48.)

Because Cornelius fasted and prayed, he, his family, and some of his friends gained eternal salvation.

Many Churches
Acts 14:23, 20:28

Acts 14:23:

"So when they had appointed elders in every church, and prayed with fasting, they commended them to the LORD in whom they had believed."

The elders referred to in the Old Testament meant heads or rulers of tribes, cities and nations (Deuteronomy 1:13). In the gospels and the book of Acts it generally refers to the Sanhedrin. In the early church, elders were the ministers and deacons, or preaching elders and business elders of the local churches. However, not all elders were apostles

Their ministry is outlined in Acts 20:28: "Therefore take heed to yourselves and to all the flock, among which the Holy Spirit has made you overseers, to shepherd the church of God which he purchased with his own blood."

Paul Suffering for Christ
2 Corinthians 11:25-28

"Three times I was beaten with rods; once I was stoned; three times I was shipwrecked; a night and a day I have been in the deep; in jouneys often, in perils of waters, in perils of robbers, in perils of my own countrymen, in perils of the Gentiles, in perils in the city, in perils in the wilderness, in perils in the sea, in perils among false brethren; in weariness and toil, in sleeplessness often, in hunger and thirst, in fastings often, in cold and nakedness—besides the other things, what comes upon me daily: my deep concern for all the churches."

David
2 Samuel 3:31-35

2 Samuel 3:31-35

Then David said to Joab and to all the people who were with him, 'Tear your clothes, gird yourselves with sackcloth, and mourn for Abner.' And King David followed the coffin. So, they buried Abner in Hebron; and the king lifted up his voice and wept at the grave of Abner, and all the people wept. And the king sang a lament over Abner and said: 'Should Abner die as a fool dies? Your hands were not bound, nor your feet put into fetters; as a man falls before wicked men, so you fell.' Then all the people wept over him again. And when all the people came to persuade David to eat food while it was still day, David took an oath, saying, 'God do so to me, and more also, if I taste bread or anything else till the sun goes down!"

Judah
Nehemiah 9:1-4

Nehemiah 9:1-4

Now in the twenty-fourth day of this month the children of Israel were assembled with fasting, and in sackcloth, and with dust on their heads. Then those of Israelite lineage separated themselves from all foreigners; and they stood and confessed their sins and the iniquities of their fathers. And they stood up in their place and read from the Book of the Law of the LORD their God for one-fourth of the day; and for another fourth they confessed and worshiped the LORD their God. Then Jeshua, Bani, Kadmiel, Shebaniah Bani, Sherebiah, Bani, and Chenani stood on the stairs of the Levites and cried out with a loud voice to the LORD their God."

Judah
Jeremiah 36:5-6

Jeremiah 36:5-6

"And Jeremiah commanded Baruch, saying, 'I am confined, I cannot, go into the house of the LORD. You go, therefore, and read from the scroll which you have written at my instruction, the words of the LORD, in the hearing of the people in the LORD's house on the day of fasting. And you shall also read them in the hearing of all Judah who come from their cities.'"

Daniel
Daniel 9:3, 16-19, 29-27

We see in Daniel 9:3 that Daniel is intent on being heard by the LORD his God: "Then I set my face toward the LORD God to make request by prayer and supplications, with fasting, sackcloth and ashes."

Further on in this chapter of the Bible, we see swift answers to Daniel's whole- hearted seeking after God. He made several specific requests.

- "Let your anger and your fury be turned away from Your city Jerusalem" (Daniel 9:16).
- "Hear my prayer" (Daniel 9:17).
- "Hear my supplications" (Daniel 9:17).
- "Cause your face to shine upon your sanctuary" (Daniel 9:17).
- "Incline your ear to hear" (Daniel 9:18).

- "Open your eyes" (9:18).
- "See our desolations" (Daniel 9:18).
- "Forgive our sins" (Daniel 9:19).
- "Do not delay my answer" (Daniel 9:19).

Daniel 9:20-27

"Now while I was speaking, praying, and confessing my sin and the sin of my people Israel, and presenting my supplication before the LORD my God for the holy mountain of my God, yes, while I was speaking in prayer, the man Gabriel, whom I had seen in the vision at the beginning, being caused to fly swiftly, reached me about the time of the evening offering. And he informed me and talked with me, and said, 'O Daniel, I have now come forth to give you skill to understand. At the beginning of your supplications the command went out, and I have come to tell you, for you are greatly beloved; therefore, consider the matter, and understand the vision: seventy weeks are determined for your people and your holy city, to finish the transgression, to make an end of sins, to make reconciliation for iniquity, to bring in everlasting righteousness, to seal up vision and prophecy, and to anoint the Most Holy. Know, therefore and understand, that from the going forth of the command to restore and build Jerusalem, until **Messiah** the Prince, there shall be seven weeks and sixty-two weeks; the street shall be built again, and the wall, even in troublesome times. And after the sixty-two weeks Messiah shall be cut off, but not for Himself; and the people of the prince, who is to come shall destroy the city and the sanctuary. The end of it shall be a flood, and till the end of the war desolations are determined. Then He shall confirm a covenant with many for one week; but in the middle of the week, he shall bring an end to sacrifice and offering. And on the wing of abominations shall be one who makes desolate, even until the consummation, which is determined, is poured out on the desolate.

This passage reveals that Jerusalem will be rebuilt. Daniel was a man who spent time with his Father God. His prayer and fasting enabled him to understand the supernatural. This revelation honored his prayer life which yielded the depth of his relationship with God. Daniel was a true prophet.

Pharisees
Luke 18:9-14

Luke 18: 9-14

"Also He spoke this parable to some who trusted in themselves that they were righteous, and despised others: 'Two went up to the temple to pray, one a Pharisee and the other a tax collector. The Pharisee stood and prayed thus with himself,' 'God, I thank you that I am not like other men—extortioners, unjust adulterers, or even as this tax collector. I fast twice a week; I give tithes of all that I possess.' And the tax collector, standing afar off, would not so much as raise his eyes to heaven, but beat his breast, saying 'God, be merciful to me a sinner!' I tell you; this man went down to his house justified rather than the other; for every one that exalts himself will be humbled, and he who humbles himself will be exalted.'"

The Pharisees' long tradition of auspicious fasting for others to see is best exemplified in Luke 18:11-12: The Pharisee was a proud man who exalted himself and bragged about his diligence to fast and pray twice a week; and he paid tithes on all his possessions.

In Contrast, Luke 18:13, we see the how the tax collector prayed. He stood far off and did not even look to heaven, instead he beat his breast in repentance and said, "God be merciful to me a sinner!"

Jesus did not respect this type of piety. In Luke 18:14 He emphasized the fact that the proud will be humbled, and the humbled will be exalted.

Our prayer and fasting must come from the heart to be effective.

Israel
Judges 20:21, 25, 26-28, and 46-48

Israel tried to conquer the Benjamites under their own power, but we see in Judges 20:21 that they knew they needed God's help. After two battles with great losses, they decided to fast and pray. God answered and then there was great victory.

In reference to the first battle, Judges 20:21 reads, "Then the children of Benjamin came out of Gibeah, and on that day cut down to the ground twenty-two thousand men of the Israelites."

In Judges 20:25 we read about the second battle: "And Benjamin went out against them from Gibeah on the second day and cut down to the ground eighteen thousand more of the children of Israel; all these drew the sword."

After these losses Israel realized they needed God's help, so they fasted and prayed. Judges 20:26 "Then all the children of Israel, that is, all the people, went up and came to the house of God and wept. They sat there before the LORD and fasted that day until evening; and they offered burnt offerings and peace offerings before the LORD."

After they fasted and prayed, God moved on their behalf. The third day was a different story. The tide began to change in Judges 20:27-28: "So the children of Israel inquired of the LORD (the ark of the covenant of God was there in those days, and Phinehas, son of Eleazar, the son of Aaron, stood before it in those days), saying, 'Shall I yet again go out to battle against the children of my brother Benjamin, or shall I cease?' And the LORD said, 'Go up, for tomorrow I will deliver them into your hand.'"

Judges 20:46-48:

"So all who fell of Benjamin that day were twenty-five thousand men who drew the sword; all these were men of valor. But six hundred men turned and fled toward the wilderness to the rock of Rimmon, and they stayed at the rock of Rimmon for four months. And the men of Israel turned back against the children of Benjamin and struck them down with the edge of the sword from every city, men and beasts, all who were found. They also set fire to all the cities they came to.

God blessed them with a great victory. Prayer and fasting are strong weapons of warfare. The church of the living God today needs to bow their heads, fast and pray with expectant faith that God is able and willing to do the uttermost for His children. We need to wake up and stand up like our God is mighty to save, heal, and deliver in any situation or circumstance.

Israel
1 Samuel 7:5-15:

"And Samuel said, 'Gather all Israel to Mizpah, and I will pray to the LORD for you.' So, they gathered, together at Mizpah, drew water, and poured it out before the Lord. And they fasted that day, and said there, "We have sinned against the Lord." And Samuel judged the children of Israel at Mizpah. Now when the Philistines heard that the children of the Israel were gathered together at Mizpah, the lords of the Philistines went up against Israel. And when the children of Israel heard it, they were afraid of the Philistines. So the children of Israel said to Samuel, 'Do not cease to cry out to the LORD our God for us, that He may save us from the hand of the Philistines.' And Samuel took a suckling lamb and offered it as a whole burnt offering to the LORD. Then Samuel cried out to the LORD for Israel, and the LORD answered him. Now as Samuel was offering up the burnt offering, the Philistines drew near to battle against Israel. *But the LORD thundered with a loud thunder upon the Philistines that day, and so confused them that they were overcome before Israel.* And the men of Israel went out of Mizpah and pursued the Philistines and drove them back as far as below Beth Car. Then Samuel took a stone set it up between Mizpah and Shen, and called its name Ebenezer saying, 'Thus far the LORD has helped us.' So, the Philistines were subdued, and they did not come anymore into the territory of Israel. And the hand of the LORD was against the Philistines all the days of Samuel. Then the cities that the Philistines had taken from Israel, were restored to Israel, from Ekron to Gath; and Israel recovered its territory from the hands of the Philistines. Also, there was peace between Israel and the Amorites. And Samuel judged Israel all the days of his life."

Samuel was indeed a prophet and a prayer warrior. He understood the dynamic power of prayer and fasting.

David
2 Samuel 1:11-12,23,18; 1 Samuel 1:13-14; Acts 13:22

David was an unusual man as Saul had sought to kill him any times and yet he mourned his death and the death of Jonathan. How strange! How utterly unlike the natural man! To tear his clothes, fast, and mourn for a man who had made twenty-one attempts to kill him, who had sought to kill his father, mother, and other family members, and had driven him from his own country. Saul tried every conceivable way to get rid of him! However, David never responded in kind. He counted Saul equal with Jonathan in his affection. In

2 Samuel 1:23 we read "Saul and Jonathan were beloved and pleasant in their lives, and in their death they were not divided; they were swifter than eagles, and they were stronger than lions."

In this case a fast was used to promote reverence for the loss of God's anointed people. This lamentation is really a *marital ode* and one of the finest in the Old Testament. David's own sufferings are forgotten while his fervent love and and deep grief for his king and his best friend, Jonathan, are expressed. There is no bitter or revengeful word or exultation over the death of his greatest enemy, Saul. The song is about the mighty warrior, the anointed one of the LORD, the delight of his people, and the father of his beloved friend. The title of the ode in Hebrew is "The Song of the Bow." Jonathan was an archer; he was excellent with the bow. The tribe of Benjamin was noted for their use of the bow. In 2 Samuel 1:18, we read David also told "them to teach the children of Judah the *Song of the Bow*." (You may read the "Song of the Bow" in the chapter entitled Songs of Praise.)

David loved without reservation. His love did not waver in the presence of extreme hatred that Saul exhibited. He loved, in this situation, like Jesus would have. No wonder he was known as "a man after God's own heart." This was recorded in the following two scripture. In 1 Samuel 13:14, we read, "But now your kingdom shall not continue. The LORD has sought for Himself a man after His own heart, and the LORD has commanded him to be commander over His people, because you have not kept what the LORD commanded you." (The prophet Samuel is speaking this to Saul about David.) Acts 13:22: "And when He had removed him, He raised up for them David as king, to whom also He gave testimony and said, 'I have found David the son of Jesse, a man after My own heart, who will do all My will.'"

What a man of God David must have been! Only a person devoted to prayer and fasting could have that level of intimacy with God.

Darius
Daniel 6:18, 22:24

This is the story of Daniel's delivery from the lions' den.

The plot against Daniel began when King Darius set up one-hundred-twenty government officials, called satraps, over the whole kingdom. Three governors were appointed to manage the satraps to be sure that the king suffered no loss. In Daniel 6:3 we read "Then this Daniel distinguished himself above the governors and satraps, because an excellent spirit was in him; and the king gave thought to setting him over the whole realm."

So, a spirit of jealousy began to grow among the governors and the satraps. They could see that King Darius respected Daniel, so they devised an evil plan. In Daniel 6:7, we see that, "All the governors of the kingdom; administrators, straps, counselors and advisors, have consulted together to establish a royal statute and make a firm decree, that, whoever petitions any god or man for thirty days, except you, O king, shall be cast into the den of lions."

They knew that Daniel prayed three times a day to his God. And they also knew how much King Darius admired Daniel. So together they went to the King and asked him to pass a degree and sign it so that it could not be changed, according to the law of the Medes and Persians. And King Darius signed it. He had been duped by the very people who were supposed to be his advisors.

When Daniel was made aware the document had been signed, he went home. And as was his custom he went to his prayer room, opened his windows toward Jerusalem, and kneeled and prayed. He usually prayed three times a day. This day would be no different as his faith was strong and would not be denied.

These evil men got together and found Daniel praying to his God. They went straight to the king, to inform him of what they had seen. They reported that Daniel was disrespecting the king because he had violated the decree. When King Darius heard this, he was upset and "set his heart to deliver him" (Daniel 6:14). When he finally realized that he was bound to the decree he demanded to see Daniel. So they brought him to the king and cast him into the fire. "But the king spoke, saying to Daniel, Your God, whom you serve continually, He will deliver you'" (Daniel 6:16).

Daniel 6:18: "Now the king went to his palace and passed the night fasting; no musicians were brought before him. Also, his sleep went from him."

In Daniel 6:22 we read that Daniel, after being kept safe by God, said "My God sent His angel and shut the lions' mouths, so that they have not hurt me, because I was found innocent before Him; and also, O king, I have done no wrong before you."

Daniel 6:24: "And the king gave the command, and they brought those men who had accused Daniel, and they cast them into the den of lions—them, their children, and their wives; and the lions overpowered them, and broke all their bones in pieces before they ever came to the bottom of the den."

God protects his faithful servants. He is our Avenger. Here we see a textbook case of a praying servant being delivered.

Esther and Mordecai

The story of Esther and Mordecai is told in Book of Esther.

They fasted three days before she went before the King Ahasuerus to save the Jews in his Kingdom. Esther's story is told earlier in this chapter.

Many people

Matthew 15:32-39 tells the story of Jesus feeding the four thousand.

Matthew 15:32-39 "Now Jesus called His disciples to Himself, and said, 'I have compassion on the multitude, because they have now continued with Me three days, and have nothing to eat. And I do not want to send them away hungry, lest they faint on the way.' Then His disciples said to Him, 'Where could we get enough bread in the wilderness to fill such a great multitude?' Jesus said to them, 'How many loaves do you have?' And they said, 'Seven and a few little fish.' So he commanded the multitude to sit down on the ground. And he took the seven loaves and the fish, and gave thanks, broke them and gave them to His disciples; and the disciples gave to the multitude. So they all ate and were filled, and they took up seven large baskets full of the fragments that were left. Now those who ate here were four thousand men, besides women and children. And He sent away the multitude, got into the boat, and came to the region of Magdala.

This is a prime example for us to understand that, with Jesus our needs are more than met. I am overwhelmed with the teaching of the "feeding of the four thousand." What a blessing from our Father! These people had fasted for three days feasting on spiritual food; they needed physical food and God provided it.

This miracle is also discussed in Mark 8:1-10.

Paul
Acts 9:8-9,17

This is the story of Paul's blindness and a three-day fast.

Acts 9:8-9 "Then Saul arose from the ground, and when his eyes were opened, he saw no one. But they led him by the hand and brought him into Damascus. And he was three days without sight, and neither ate nor drank."

We read in Acts 9:17, that the fast came to an end: "And Ananias went his way and entered the house; and laying his hands on him, he said, 'Brother Saul, the LORD Jesus, who appeared to you on the road as you came, has sent me that you may receive your sight and be filled with the Holy Spirit.'" "And Ananias went his way and entered the house; and laying his hands on him, he said, 'Brother Saul, the LORD Jesus, who appeared to you on the road as you came, has sent me that you may receive your sight and be filled with the Holy Spirit.'"

This is an example of a fast that led to a spiritual breakthrough for Paul.

David
2 Samuel 12:16-23

David is grieving the impending death of his first, child conceived with Bathsheba:

David pleaded with God for the life for the child, and David fasted and went in, and lay all night on the ground. So the elders of his house went to him, to raise him from the ground. But he would not, nor did he eat bread with them. Then on the seventh day it came to pass that the child died. And the servants of David were afraid to tell him that the child was dead. For they said, 'Indeed, while the child was alive, we spoke to him, and he would not heed our voice. How can we tell him that the child is dead? He may do some harm!' When David saw that his servants were whispering, he perceived that the child was dead. David said to his servants, 'Is the child dead?' and they said, 'He is dead.' So David arose from the ground, washed and anointed himself, changed his clothes; and went into the house of the LORD and worshipped. Then he went to his own house; and when he requested, they set food before him, and he ate (2 Samuel 12:16-23).

David's faith did not falter, but he believed God despite the death of his child. David did not question the fact that that he had fasted and prayed for the child to live to no avail. David's trust in God enabled him to accept the will of his Father.

This is a great example of his faith in God. The prayer and fasting were not in vain. They proved to David that God's perfect will had been done.

Israel
1 Samuel 31:2-6, 8-13 tells of the rescue of Saul's body.

Then the Philistines followed hard after Saul and his sons. And the Philistines killed Jonathan, Abinadab, and Malchishua, Saul's sons. The battle became fierce against Saul. The archers hit him, and he was severely wounded by the archers. Then Saul said to his armorbearer, 'Draw your sword, and thrust me through with it, lest these uncircumcised men come and thrust me through and abuse me.' But his armorbearer would not, for he was greatly afraid. Therefore, Saul took a sword and fell on it. And when his armorbearer saw that Saul was dead, he also fell on his sword and died with him. So Saul, his three sons, his armorbearer, and all his men died together that same day (1 Samuel 31:2-6).

So, it happened the next day, when the Philistines came to strip the slain, that they found Saul and his three sons fallen on Mount Gilboa. And they cut off his head and stripped off his armor, and sent word throughout the land of the Philistines, to proclaim it in the temple of their idols and among the people. Then they put his armor in the temple of the Ashtoreth, and they fastened his body to the wall of Beth Shan. (Ashtoreth was the female counterpart of Baal.) Now when the inhabitants of Jabesh Gilead heard what the Philistines had done to Saul, all the valiant men arose and traveled all night, and took the body of Saul and the bodies of his sons from the wall of Beth Shan; and they came to Jabesh and burned them there. Then they took their bones and buried them under the tamarisk tree at Jabesh and fasted seven days" (1 Samuel 31:8-13).

They fasted for seven days after they burned the bodies and buried their bones. They were mourning the deaths of these brave men and the cruel way their bodies had been treated. It was not their custom to burn dead bodies; however, they did it to keep their bodies from being further desecrated. They were also praying for the families of Saul and his three sons. They were grieving about the sudden death of their loved ones.

Paul and Seventy-Six Men

Acts 27:9-10: "Now when much time had been spent, and when sailing was now dangerous because the Fast was already over, Paul advised them, saying, 'Men, I perceive that this voyage will end with disaster and much loss, not only of the cargo and ship, but also our lives.

They sailed on anyway and got into treacherous weather.

Acts 27:21-26, we read:

But after long abstinence from food, then Paul stood in the midst of them and said, 'Men, you should have listened to me, and not have sailed from Crete and incurred this disaster and loss. And now I urge you to take heart, for there will be no loss of life among you, but only of the ship. For there stood by me this night an angel of the God to whom I belong and whom I serve, saying, 'Do not be afraid Paul; you must be brought before Caesar; and indeed, God has granted you all those who sail with you.' Therefore, take heart, men, for I believe God that it will be just as it was told me. However, we must run aground on a certain island.'"

Acts 27:33 states: "And as day was about to dawn, Paul implored them all to take food, saying, 'Today is the fourteenth day that you have waited and continued without food, having eaten nothing.'"

It was terrible! The ship ran aground and broke apart. However, everyone made it safely to land. There were two hundred and seventy-six men on the ship. The lives of the men were saved because Paul was faithful to fast and pray.

Daniel
Daniel 10:2-14 tells the story of Daniel's fast and vision:

In those days I, Daniel, was mourning three full weeks. I ate no pleasant food, no meat or wine came into my mouth, nor did I anoint myself at all, till three whole weeks were fulfilled. Now on the twenty-fourth day of the first month, as I was by the side of the great river, that is, the Tigris, I lifted my eyes and looked, and behold, a certain man clothed in linen, whose waist was girded with gold of Uphaz! His body was like beryl, his face like the appearance of lightning, his eyes like torches of fire, his arms and feet like burnished bronze in color, and the sound of his words like the voice of a multitude. And I, Daniel, alone saw the vision, for the men who were with me did not see the vision; but a great terror fell upon them, so that they fled to hide themselves. Therefore, I was left alone when I saw this great vision, and no strength remained in me; for my vigor was turned to frailty in me, and I retained no strength. Yet, I heard the sound of his words; and while I heard the sound of his words I was in a deep sleep on my face, with my face to the ground. Suddenly, a hand touched me, which made me tremble on my knees and the palms of my hands. And he said to me, "O Daniel, man greatly beloved, understand the words that I speak to you, and stand upright, for I have now been sent to you." While he was speaking this word to me, I stood trembling. Then he said to me, "Do not fear, Daniel, for from the first day that you set your heart to understand, and to humble yourself before your God, your words were heard, and I have come because of your words. But the prince of the kingdom of Persia withstood me twenty-one days; and behold, Michael, one of the chief princes, came to help me, for I had been left alone there with the kings of Persia. Now I have come to make you understand what will happen to your people in the latter days, for the vision refers to many days yet to come."

In Daniel 10:13 we find spiritual warfare in progress. The prince of Persia is the chief ruler of demonic powers fighting on behalf of Persians gods. Michael, the archangel, was sent to lead the battle against the evil forces. The exact cause of this battle and the reason why the messenger could not bring victory are not discussed. Michael settled that issue, bringing assistance.

This passage of scripture states clearly that demonic armies oppose God's plans and purposes. We can now understand that earthly struggles often mirror what is happening in the heavens. This further calls us to prayer and fasting to pray against these forces. It encourages us to remain vigilant in prayer and to continue until the answer comes.

Moses

Deuteronomy 9:9 - 10-10 tells of Moses's three forty-day fasts.

Moses's first forty day fast

Deuteronomy 9:9-21:

When I went up into the mountain to receive the tables of stone, the tables of the covenant which the LORD made with you, then I stayed on the mountain forty days and forty nights. I neither ate bread nor drank water. Then the LORD delivered unto me two tables of stone written with the finger of God, and on them were all the words which the LORD had spoken to you on the mountain from the midst of the fire in the day of the assembly. And it came to pass after forty days and forty nights that the LORD gave me the two tablets of stone, the tablets of the covenant. Then the LORD said to me, 'Arise, go down quickly from here, for your people whom you brought out of Egypt have acted corruptly; they have quickly turned aside from the way which I commanded them; they have made themselves a molded image.' Furthermore, the LORD spoke to me, saying, 'I have seen this people, and indeed they are a stiff-necked (stubborn and obstinate) people. Let Me alone, that I may destroy them and blot out their name from under heaven; and I will make you a nation mightier and greater than they.' So, I turned and came down the mountain, and the mountain burned with fire; and the two tablets of the covenant were in my two hands. And I looked and behold, you had sinned against the LORD your God—had made for yourselves a molded calf! You had turned aside quickly from the way which the LORD had commanded you. Then I took the two tablets and threw them out of my two hands and broke them before your eyes. And I fell down before the LORD, as at the first, forty days and forty nights; I neither ate bread nor drank water because of all your sin which you committed in doing wickedly in the sight of the LORD, to provoke Him to anger. For I was afraid of the anger and hot displeasure with which the LORD was angry with you, to destroy you. But the LORD listened to me at that time also. And the LORD was very angry with Aaron and would have destroyed him; so, I prayed for Aaron also at the same time. Then I took your sin, the calf which you had made, and burned it with fire and crushed it and ground it very small, until it was as fine as dust; and I threw its dust into the brook that descended from the mountain."

Moses' second forty-day fast and the second set of tablets of stone

Deuteronomy 9:25-26: "Thus I prostrated myself before the LORD; forty days and forty nights I kept prostrating myself, because the LORD had said He would destroy you. Therefore,

I prayed to the LORD, and said: 'O LORD God, do not destroy Your people and Your inheritance whom You have redeemed through Your greatness, whom You have brought out of Egypt with a mighty hand.'"

Deuteronomy 9:29: "Yet they are Your people and Your inheritance, whom You brought out by Your mighty power and by Your outstretched arm."

Deuteronomy 10:1-5: "At that time the LORD said unto me, 'Hew for yourself two tablets of stone like the first and come up to Me on the mountain and make yourself an ark of wood. And I will write on the tablets the words that were on the first tablets, which you broke; and you shall put them in the ark.' So I made an ark of acacia wood, hewed two tablets of stone like the first, and went up the mountain having the two tablets in my hand. And He wrote on the tablets according to the first writing, the Ten Commandments, which the LORD had spoken to you in the mountain from the midst of the fire in the day of the assembly; and the LORD gave them to Me. Then I turned and came down from the mountain and put the tablets in the ark which I had made; and there they are, just as the LORD commanded me."

Deuteronomy 10:8: "At that time the LORD separated the tribe of Levi to bear the ark of the covenant of the LORD, to stand before the LORD to minister to Him, and to bless in His name, to this day."

Moses' third forty-day fast

Deuteronomy 10-11: "As at the first time, I stayed in the mountain forty days and forty nights; the LORD also heard me at that time, and the LORD chose not to destroy you. Then the LORD said to me, 'Arise, begin your journey before the people, that they may go in and possess the land, which I swore to their fathers to give them.'"

Moses, a great man of God! He saw the power of prayer and fasting. The Israelites were spared the wrath of God, and they received His commandments, written by His own hand.

Joshua
Exodus 24:13, 32:17-19

Joshua was with Moses on the mountain for the first forty-day fast.

Exodus 24:13: "So Moses arose with his assistant Joshua, and Moses went up to the mountain of God."

Exodus 32:17-19:

And when Joshua heard the noise of the people as they shouted, he said to Moses, *"There is noise of war in the camp."* (And it was so—it was spiritual war!) But he (Moses) said, "It is not the noise of the shout of victory, nor the noise of the cry of defeat, but the sound of singing I hear." So it was, as soon as he came near the camp, that he saw the calf and the dancing. So, Moses' anger became hot, and he cast the tablets out of his hands and broke them at the foot of the mountain.

Joshua was the man that God had chosen to lead them into the promised land. He would have seen firsthand the necessity of prayer and fasting to spiritual breakthrough and practical victory of every kind.

Elijah

Elijah was fleeing from Jezebel who threatened to kill him because he had killed all the prophets of Baal at Mt. Carmel - all 850 of them. He traveled a day's journey and sat under a juniper tree (a well-known tree of the cedar family) and he prayed "Now, LORD, take my life for I am no better than my fathers!"

1 Kings 19: 6-8

And he looked, and there by his head was a cake baked on coals, and a jar of water. So he ate and drank and lay down again. And the angel of the LORD came back the second time, and touched him, and said, 'Arise and eat, because the journey is too great for you.' So he arose, and ate and drank; and he went in the *strength of that food forty days and forty nights* as far as Horeb, the mountain of God.

Mount Horeb is another name for Mt. Sinai, which was about 200 miles from Beersheba. Elijah was going to the very place where the LORD had revealed himself to Moses and the children of Israel.

God then revealed Himself to Elijah as we read in 1 Kings 19:11-13:

Then He said, 'Go out, and stand on the mountain before the LORD.' And behold, the LORD passed by, and a great and strong wind tore into the mountains and broke the rocks in pieces before the LORD, but the LORD was not in the wind; and after the wind an earthquake, but the LORD was not in the earthquake; and after the earthquake a fire, but the LORD was not in the fire; and after the fire a still small voice. So it was, when Elijah heard it, that he wrapped his face in his mantle and went out and stood in the entrance of the cave. Suddenly a voice came to him, and said, 'What are you doing here, Elijah?"

1 Kings 19:15-16: "Then the LORD said to him: 'Go, return on your way to the Wilderness of Damascus, and when you arrive, anoint Hazael as king over Syria. Also, you shall anoint Jehu the son of Nimshi as king over Israel, and Elisha the son of Shaphat of Abel Meholah you shall anoint as prophet in your place.'"

Elijah fasted and prayed. The LORD was faithful to guide him very specifically. Additionally, he was blessed with the physical presence of God because of his dedication.

Jesus

This is the story of Jesus being tempted in the wilderness.

In Matthew 4:1-4, we read: "Then Jesus was led up by the Spirit into the wilderness to be tempted by the devil. And when He had fasted *forty days and forty nights,* afterward He was hungry. Now when the tempter came to Him, he said, 'If You are the Son of God, command that these stones become bread.' But He answered and said, 'It is written Man shall not live by bread alone, but by every word that proceeds from the mouth of God.

In Matthew 4:10-11, we read: "Then Jesus said to him, 'Away with you, Satan! For it is written, you shall worship the LORD your God, and Him only you shall serve.' Then the devil left Him, and behold, angels came and ministered to Him.

Jesus is our ultimate example. If He fasted for connection with God and power from on high, then so should we.

CHAPTER 3
Seeking God

Matthew 6:33: "But seek first the kingdom of God and His righteousness, and all these things shall be added to you."

Seeking God involves so many things, but simply put, it is focusing our hearts and minds on God and what He may be saying to us or doing in our lives.

Hannah: A God Seeker

God wants us to seek Him with all our hearts and surely, we will find Him. He says to us, "Seek Me" like Hannah did with such fervor that the priest thought she was drunk. However, she was a barren woman in travail yearning for her womb to be filled with child. She promised God that she would give her first-born son to serve Him all the days of his life and that she would take him to the temple at the appropriate time. She prayed until the answer came. She pressed into God, and He gave her Samuel and filled her womb with many more children. After Samuel was born Hannah bore three more sons and two daughters for a grand total of six babies.

1 Samuel 1:9-28:

So Hannah arose after she had finished eating and drinking in Shiloh. Now Eli the priest was sitting on the seat by the doorpost of the tabernacle of the LORD. And she was in bitterness of soul and prayed to the LORD and wept in anguish. Then she made a vow and said, 'O LORD of Hosts, if You will indeed look on the affliction of Your maidservant and remember me, and do not forget Your maidservant, but will give your maidservant a male child, then I will give him to the LORD all the days of his life and no razor shall come upon his head.' And it happened, as she continued praying before the LORD, that Eli watched her mouth. Now Hannah spoke in her heart; only her lips moved, but her voice was not heard. Therefore Eli thought she was drunk. So Eli said to her, 'How long will you be drunk? Put your wine away from you!' But Hannah answered and said, 'No, my lord, I am a woman of sorrowful spirit, I have drunk neither wine nor intoxicating drink, but have poured out my soul before the LORD. Do not consider your maidservant a wicked woman, but out of the abundance of my complaint and grief I have spoken until now.' Then Eli answered and said, 'Go in peace, and the God of Israel grant your petition which you have asked of Him.' And she said, 'Let your maidservant find favor in your sight.' So the woman went her way and ate, and her face was no longer sad. Then they rose early in the morning and worshiped before the LORD and returned and came to their house in Ramah. And Elkanah knew Hannah his wife, and the LORD remembered her. So it came to pass in the process of time that Hannah conceived and bore a son, and called his name Samuel, saying 'Because I have asked for Him from the LORD.' Now the man Elkanah and all his house went up to offer to the LORD the yearly sacrifice and his vow. But Hannah did not go up, for she said to her husband, 'Not until the child is weaned; then I will take him, that he may appear before the LORD and remain there forever.' So Elkanah her husband said to her, 'Do what seems best to you; wait until you have weaned him. Only let the LORD establish His word.' Then the woman stayed and nursed her son until she had weaned him." Now when she had weaned him, she took him up with her, with three bulls, one ephah of flour, and a skin of wine, and brought him to the house of the LORD in Shiloh. And the child was young. (Samuel was probably five years old.) Then they slaughtered a bull and brought the child to Eli. And she said 'O my LORD! As your soul lives, my lord, I am the woman who stood by you here, praying to the LORD. For this child I prayed, and the LORD has granted me my petition which I asked of Him. Therefore, I also have lent him the LORD; as long as he lives, he shall be lent to the LORD.' So they worshiped the LORD there.

Hannah prayed the most beautiful prayer in 2 Samuel 2:1-10. To appreciate this prayer, one must understand the great pain and sorrow barren Hebrew women bore. Hannah felt alone, an outcast, and disgraced. This was a result of the shaming she felt before becoming a mother. In the profound words spoken by Dr. Joel Baden: "The experience of infertility in ancient Israel was utterly crushing."[1] Rachael expressed this feeling at the birth of Joseph her first child. Genesis 30:23

reads "And she conceived and bore a son and said, 'God has taken away my reproach (disgrace).'"

Hannah had the added burden of seeing Peninnah, Elkanah's other wife, with her children. Peninnah was severely unkind to Hannah, callously causing her more heartache and pain because the LORD had closed her womb. Hannah's prayer is from her heart. She is praising and smiling at her enemies (Peninnah). We see in 1 Samuel 2:5 "Even the barren has borne seven, and she who has many children has become feeble." This is a direct reference to Peninnah.

Hannah rejoiced and thanked God that *He* had taken her pain and turned it to joy. This reminded me of what David said in Psalm 30:1: "I will, extol You, O LORD for You have lifted me up, and have not let my foes rejoice over me." He continues in verse eleven, "You have turned for me my mourning into dancing; You have put off my sackcloth and clothed me with gladness." God is our sovereign God, and we can trust Him.

God can take the direst circumstances and make them the greatest victories.

1 Samuel 2:18-21:

"But Samuel ministered before the LORD, even as a child, wearing a linen ephod. Moreover, his mother used to make him a little robe, and bring it to him year by year when she came up with her husband to offer the yearly sacrifice. And

Eli would bless Elkanah and his wife and say, 'The LORD give you descendants from this woman for the loan that was given to the LORD.' Then they would go to their own home. And the LORD visited Hannah, so that she conceived and bore three sons and two daughters. Meanwhile the child Samuel grew before the LORD."

Hannah was a God seeker and God gave her Samuel, who was a God-seeker. He was an outstanding prophet, and he was also treated like a king, because the Israelite nation revered him. Hannah's persistent seeking of God led to a remarkable life in which faith was rewarded and her story was recorded in scripture for centuries of believers to read and draw strength from. Hannah's "Song of Prayer" is included in chapter ten.

Moses: A God Seeker

Moses was a God seeker. The results were phenomenal in the realm of miracles and revealed in the strength of his leadership as well as in the history of Israel. This story begins with Moses living in a house with his parents, floating in a basket on the Nile River, and finally residing in the house of Pharaoh. Pharaoh's daughter saw baby Moses and took him to her home. She adopted him and he became Pharaoh's grandson. He grew up with plenty and became the leader of the nation of Israel. Moses led them out of Egyptian bondage through the wilderness to receive the Ten Commandments on Mt. Sinai. Moses died on Mount Nebo. In Deuteronomy 34:7 we read "Moses was one hundred twenty-years old when he died. His eyes were not dim nor his natural vigor diminished."

Moses had an intimate relationship with God as is referenced in Deuteronomy 34:10 "But since then there has not arisen in Israel a prophet like Moses, whom the LORD knew face to face."

Because Moses had laid his hands on Joshua, the children of Israel respected Joshua and did as the LORD commanded them. He led them into the promised land.

Moses is listed in the hall of faith recorded in scripture. Hebrews 11:23-26 we read:

By faith Moses, when he was born, was hidden three months by his parents, because they saw he was a beautiful child; and they were not afraid of the king's command. By faith Moses, when he became of age, refused to be called the son of Pharaoh's daughter, choosing rather to suffer affliction with the people of God than to enjoy the passing pleasures of sin, esteeming the reproach of Christ greater riches than the pleasures in Egypt; for he looked to the reward.

He chose the reward of serving the LORD and looking toward a messianic future.

Jochebed, mother of Moses, was a Levite and a very vigilant mother. It was her brave action that saved his life. However, the child she delivered would later deliver her and the nation of Israel out of Egyptian bondage to the promised land.

Down through the ages God has called God seekers to their knees to taste and see that He is good! And oh! He is so, so good.

Early will we seek Him, to know Him, to love Him, to praise Him and to receive from His bounty and to share His message with His people. This should be the cry of our hearts.

We must be messengers of hope, peace, and love from the Prince of Peace, Jesus–Jesus, our precious Jesus, who died on a cruel cross for us. He was, is, and will always be the powerful Son of God. He walked this earth, was crucified, dead, and buried and three days later he arose from the grave. He bought our salvation.

The Bible tells us to seek God with our whole hearts.

Psalm 119:2: "Blessed are those who keep His testimonies, who seek Him with a whole heart!"

2 Chronicles 15:12 "Then they entered into a covenant to seek the LORD God of their fathers with all their heart and with all their soul."

2 Chronicles 15:15 "And all Judah rejoiced at the oath, for they had sworn with all their heart and sought Him with all their soul; and He was found by them, and the LORD gave them rest all around." Praise His holy name!

In Luke 2:25-32, we find Simeon and in Luke 2:36-38 we find Anna, the prophetess. These two servants of God were found in the temple enjoying the distinct and holy privilege of seeing the Messiah in person, the baby Jesus with his parents, Mary and Joseph. Simeon and Anna were aging saints of God who had prayed to see the Messiah. The prayer of their hearts was answered. They were two great God seekers that little is written about; however, much was said about in a few powerful words. God loved them so much that He recorded it in scriptures for all to read.

God seekers are special to God. They are called. First, God must seek them, and they must answer His call to receive his Son. They must begin to *mine* the treasures of His word and seek after Him often in prayer. When He sees their great love for Him; He calls them to be God seekers, intercessors, devoted only to God for all to know Him, to love Him, and to become a part of His kingdom.

Seeking the LORD means seeking His presence. *Presence* is a common translation of the Hebrew word "face." So, this is the Hebraic way of having access to God. To be before His face is to be in His presence.

Aren't we always in His presence? Yes, but there are times in which God's tangible presence is not evident. This is the reason that the Bible constantly calls us to "seek the LORD... seek His presence continually." God's manifest, conscious, trusted presence is not our constant experience. There are seasons when we become neglectful of God and give Him no thought and do not put our trust in Him; therefore, we do not find him manifested in our prayer lives. We do not perceive Him as great, beautiful and valuable in the eyes of our hearts. At this point, His face—the brightness of His person—is hidden behind the curtain of our carnal desire. This condition is always ready to overtake us. That is why we are told to "seek His presence continually."

The Bible tells us in 1 Chronicles. 22:19: "Now set your heart and your soul to seek the LORD your God." And in Colossians, 3:1-2 we read: "If then you were raised with Christ, seek those things that are above, where Christ is, sitting at the right hand of God. Set your mind on things above, not on things on the earth."

Seeking God is a constant choice. It is the setting of your mind, a conscious choice to direct your heart toward God. Paul wrote in 2 Thessalonians 3:5: "Now may the LORD direct your hearts into the love of God and into the patience of Christ." This effort is a gift from God. It is not a natural inclination. A heart that is specially called to be an intercessor has a heart not only to seek, but to keep on seeking until the answer comes, keep on knocking until the burden lifts, keep on praying until the power falls. Perseverance of this depth is from God and God alone. It is an awesome call, "For many are called, but few are chosen" (Matthew 22:14).

This kind of seeking is the conscious effort to get through the natural means to God Himself; to constantly set our minds toward God in all our experiences, to direct our hearts and minds toward Him through the means of His revelation and to pierce the veil of the natural to enter the realm of the supernatural.

Blessings for seeking God:

- **We will find Him.** Jeremiah. 29:13: "And you will seek Me and find Me, when you search for Me with all your heart." The LORD continues in this portion of Jeremiah: 29:14 to say, "I will be found by you."
- **The LORD will be good to us.** Lamentations 3:25: "The LORD is good to those who wait for Him, to the soul who seeks Him."
- **We will lack no good thing.** Psalm 34:10: "The young lions lack and suffer hunger, but those who seek the LORD shall not lack any good thing."
- **We will be delivered from fear.** Psalm. 34:4: "I sought the LORD and He heard me and delivered me from all my fears."
- **We will have success.** 2 Chronicles 26:5: "He (Uzziah) sought God in the days of Zechariah, who had understanding in the visions of God, and as long as He sought the LORD, God made him prosper."
- **He will never forsake us.** Psalm 9:10: "And those who know Your name will put their trust in You; for You, LORD have not forsaken those who seek You."
- **We will be blessed and happy.** Psalm 119:2: "Blessed are those who keep His testimonies and seek Him with the whole heart!"

Isaiah tells us in 55:6-7: "Seek the LORD while He may be found, call upon Him while He is near. Let the wicked forsake his way, and the unrighteous man his thoughts; let him return to the LORD, and He will have mercy on him; and to our God, for He will abundantly pardon."

In 1Chronicles 16:11 we see a direct command: "Seek the LORD and His strength; seek His face evermore!"

David wrote in Psalm 105:4: "Seek the LORD and His strength; seek His face evermore!"

Do we realize we have a command to seek God? There are people in this world who seek many things such as fame, wealth, influence, and power, but there are not too many people who really seek God. Yet, seeking God must be man's most glorious moment. It is worship to our Father, God.

One of the problems in seeking God is that by His very nature He is hidden from us. This is partially due to our own sinfulness. This is supported by scripture in Isaiah 59:1-2: "Behold the LORD's hand is not shortened, that it cannot save; nor His ear heavy, that it cannot hear. But your iniquities have separated you from Your God; and your sins have hidden His face from you, so that He will not hear."

There is another reason why God is sometimes hidden. It is due to His own mysterious nature. Isaiah laments: "Truly You are a God who hides Yourself, O God of Israel, the Savior" (Isaiah 45:15)! We read in the Psalms that "Clouds and darkness surround Him; righteousness and justice are the foundation of His throne"(Psalm 97:2).

It is stated in Exodus 20:21: "So the people stood afar off, but Moses drew near the thick darkness where God was." Is this a paradox that the God of blinding light is surrounded with thick darkness?

No. God is God and can represent Himself in any form that He chooses. It could be that we must have the boldness of Moses to pursue God with great faith through the darkness. It takes a close relationship with God to do this. Moses understood God and trusted Him with all His heart. We know because we have experienced God in the darkest places of our soul. He is always near to those who are have a broken heart and a contrite spirit.

David affirms this fact in Psalm 34:18: "The LORD is near to those who have a broken heart and saves such as have a contrite spirit."

David: A God Seeker:

How will we respond to God's command to seek Him? Will we respond like David? He was a great seeker of God. In his search for God, he cried out: *"When You said, 'Seek My face,' My heart said to You, 'Your face, LORD, I will seek'"* (Psalm 27:8).

God gave David a kingdom that would last forever because He sought the LORD.

Hezekiah, a God Seeker:

The Bible speaks of many seekers. Let us now consider Hezekiah. He was a God seeker in the Old Testament. King Hezekiah is going to bless us as we see the depth of his relationship with Almighty God. Let us search the treasures in God's word about Hezekiah. Who was he? His father was Ahaz and his mother was Abi, daughter of Zechariah. Hezekiah was and in the Messianic line of Jesus. He was often called the son of David. The name Hezekiah in Hebrew is translated *God Is My Strength*. He lived up to his name. He became king of Judah at the age of twenty-five and remained on the throne for twenty-nine years. He was the greatest of all Judaean kings. After David, he was perhaps the most righteous and faithful king that reigned in Judah.

Hezekiah succeeded his idolatrous father Ahaz, who ruled a kingdom discontented with both the religious and political situations into which his father had led them. King Ahaz had made alliances with heathen nations such as Assyria, Moab, Edom, Philistia, Ethiopia and others. As a result he closed the temple and boarded up its doors. He also placed altars throughout the city honoring the heathen gods. Sennacharib, King of Assyria, appears to have been the leader of the heathen coalition that Ahaz had joined.

Hezekiah began his leadership as king with reopening and cleansing the temple of all the Assyrian cult matter which his father had introduced, thus breaking this alliance. Ahaz had compromised Judah with his bond to these godless kingdoms.

He restored the temple and worship by cleansing the temple from all ungodliness. He is greatly remembered for this act as a newly crowned king. It was in the third year of Hoshea, King of Israel, that Hezekiah began his reign as King of Judah.

This scripture is recorded in 2 Kings 18:3-6:

"And he did what was right in the sight of the LORD, according to all that his father David had done. He removed the high places, and broke the sacred pillars, cut down the wooden image, and broke in pieces the bronze serpent that Moses had made; for until those days the children of Israel burned incense to it, and called it Nehushtan. He trusted in the LORD God of Israel, so that after him was none like him among all the kings of Judah, nor who were before him. For he held fast to the LORD; he did not depart from following Him, but kept His commandments, which the LORD had commanded Moses."

This was Hezekiah's first act as king, and it revealed his passion for God.

This Hezekiah's second act of kingship was also very extraordinary. This second act of mercy for Judah must be explained before discussed. His father, Ahaz, had made an alliance with the ancient Assyrian Empire. At that time, it was the most powerful empire in the world. For three hundred years, from 900 - 600 BC, the Assyrian Empire expanded, conquered and ruled the Middle East, including Mesopotamia, Egypt and the coast of Asia Minor - which is known as Turkey. This ancient empire grew through military conquest to cover a huge region that encompassed today's Iran, Iraq, Armenia, Afghanistan, Turkey, Bulgaria, many parts of Greece, Egypt, Syria, much of what is now Pakistan, Jordan, Israel, the West Bank, the Gaza Strip, Lebanon, Caucasia, Central Asia, Libya and the northern parts of Arabia. It was a vast empire.

Sennacherib reigned as king of the empire during this period when Ahaz and Hezekiah ruled Judah. To understand how great the miracle we are about to discuss was, we must realize that Judah was a small kingdom comprised of only two tribes of Israel and were more or less subjected to this huge empire since the reign of Ahaz. This empire was steeped in pagan worship; thus, Ahaz closed the temple doors and installed altars to these pagan gods because he had bowed his knee to king Sennacharib's way of life.

We see Hezekiah's dramatic conflict with Sennacharib in 2 Kings 18:13-16:

And in the fourteenth year of King Hezekiah, Sennacherib, King of Assyria came up against all the fortified cities of Judah and took them. Then Hezekiah, king of Judah, sent to the king of Assyria at Lachish, saying, 'I have done wrong; turn away from me; whatever you impose on me I will pay.' And the king of Assyria assessed Hezekiah king of Judah three hundred talents of silver and thirty talents of gold. So Hezekiah gave him all the silver that was found in the house of the LORD and in the treasuries of the king's house. At that time Hezekiah stripped the gold from the doors of the temple of the LORD, and from the pillars which Hezekiah, king of Judah, had overlaid, and gave it to the king of Assyria."

Immediately following this encounter, the king of Assyria sent three military chiefs with a strong military force to king Hezekiah in Jerusalem. In 2 Kings 18:19-22, we read:

Then *the* Rabshakeh, (the chief spokesman), said to them, 'Say now to Hezekiah, 'Thus says the great king, the king of Assyria: What confidence is this in which you trust? You speak of having plans and power for war; but they are mere words. And in whom do you trust that you rebel against me? Now look! You are trusting in the staff of this broken reed, Egypt, on which if a man leans, it will go into his hand and pierce it. So is Pharaoh king of Egypt to all who trust in him. But if you say to me, 'We trust in the LORD our God,' is it not He whose high places and whose altars Hezekiah has taken away, and said to Judah and Jerusalem,'You shall worship before this altar in Jerusalem?'"

And in 2 Kings 18:25, he continued to boast against the LORD saying, "Have I now come up without the LORD against this place to destroy it? The LORD has said to me, 'Go up against this land and destroy it.'"

Eliakim, who oversaw Hezekiah's palace, asked, "'Please speak to your servants in Aramaic, for we understand it; and do not speak to us in Hebrew in the hearing of the people who are on the wall" (2 Kings 18:26).

However, Rabshakeh continued his rant explaining that it was not a private message, it was a message for everyone. If they did not come to terms with their enemy, they would be eating their own waste and drinking their own urine with Hezekiah. "But do not listen to Hezekiah, lest he persuade you, saying, 'The LORD will deliver us'"(2 Kings 18:32).

The people's response was silence. Not one word was spoken as king Hezekiah had instructed them saying, "Do not answer him"(2 Kings 18:36). Eliakim, Shebna, and Joah went back to King Hezekiah with their clothes torn and reported all of this to him. When he heard what had been said he tore his robes and dressed in sackcloth and went to the house of the LORD. Then he sent Eliakim and Shebna and all the senior priests dressed in sackcloth to Isaiah, the prophet. They described to Isaiah what a terrible blasphemy against God had been committed by the Assyrians and what terrible disrespect they had shown for God by their evil talk. They asked Isaiah to pray for what was left of the people.

Isaiah told them to tell Hezekiah not to be concerned at what their enemy said would happen, stressing, in essence, that there were all outrageous blasphemies. God promised, through the prophet Isaiah, that he would make the Assyrians second-guess themselves and put them into a state of self-doubt. The king of Assyria would hear a rumor, become frightened for his life, and return to his own country. Once there, he would be killed.

Sennacherib sent another envoy with a letter to Hezekiah containing more threats against Jerusalem and Judah. He read the letter, went to the temple and spread it before the Lord. He then prayed.

We read his prayer in 2 Kings 19:15-19:

'O LORD God of Israel, the One who dwells between the cherubim, You are

God, You alone, of all the kingdoms of the earth. You have made heaven and earth. Incline Your ear, O LORD, and hear; open Your eyes, O LORD, and see; and hear the words of Sennacherib, which he has sent to reproach the living God. Truly, LORD, the kings of Assyria have laid waste the nations and their lands and have cast their gods into the fire; for they were not gods, but the work of men's hands—wood and stone. Therefore, they destroyed them. Now therefore, O LORD our God, I pray, save us from his hand, that all the kingdoms of the earth may know that You are the LORD God, You alone.'

The scripture passage of 2 Kings 19:8–9 demonstrates the fact that physical acts combined with prayer and faith bring success. In 2 Kings 19:14 we see that King Hezekiah received a threatening letter "from the hand of enemy messengers, and he read it; and Hezekiah went up to the house of the LORD, and spread it before the LORD." His physical act of taking the letter to the LORD established his faith and trust in God.

It became the foundation of faith that Hezekiah stood upon as he prayed. Almighty God answered his prayer with a *great victory, in a miraculous way.*

In 2 Kings 19:35-37 we read:

And it came to pass on a certain night that the angel of the LORD went out and killed in the camp of the Assyrians one hundred and eighty-five thousand; and when the people arose early in the morning, there were the corpses—all dead. So Sennacherib, king of Assyria departed and went away, returned home, and remained at Nineveh. Now it came to pass, as he was worshipping in the temple of Nisroch, his god, that his sons Adrammelech and Sharezer struck him down with the sword; and they escaped into the land of Ararat. Then Esarhaddon his son reigned in his place.

Hezekiah exhibited great faith and was motivated by a genuine intensity of prayer-passion. He sought the LORD and God Almighty fought the battle for him. Our God never fails us.

Hezekiah approached every event with prayer and faith. He was truly a God seeker and God answered him many times over.

Later Hezekiah became sick and Isaiah went to see him. The news was not good. This is recorded in 2 Kings 20:1-11:

Thus says the LORD: 'Set your house in order for you shall die and not live.' Then he turned his face toward the wall, and prayed to the LORD saying, 'Remember now, O LORD, I pray, how I have walked before You in truth and with a loyal heart and have done what was good in Your sight.' And Hezekiah wept bitterly. And it happened before Isaiah had gone out into the middle court, that the word of the LORD came to him saying, 'Return and tell Hezekiah the leader of My people, 'Thus says the LORD, the God of David your father: 'I have heard your prayer, I have seen your tears; surely I will heal you. On the third day you shall go up to the house of the LORD. And I will add to your days fifteen years. I will deliver you and this city from the hand of the king of Assyria; and I will defend this city for My own sake and for the sake of My servant David.' Then Isaiah said, 'Take a lump of figs.' So they took and laid it on the boil, and he recovered. And Hezekiah said to Isaiah, 'What is the sign that the LORD will heal me, and that I shall go up to the house of the LORD the third day?' Then Isaiah said, 'This is the sign to you from the LORD, that the LORD will do the thing which He has spoken: 'Shall the shadow go forward ten degrees or go backward ten degrees?' (God gave Hezekiah a choice.) And Hezekiah answered, "It is an easy thing for the shadow to go down ten degrees; no, but let the shadow go backward ten degrees. So Isaiah the prophet cried out to the LORD, and He brought the shadow ten degrees backward, by which it had gone down on the sundial of Ahaz."

Hezekiah was a devoted prayer warrior. God listened intently to his prayers. Perhaps because he walked a faith-filled walk, stood for righteousness and did not waver in the face of great trials. He turned *boldly* to God expecting to see God be God, and God never *failed* him.

The fact that God gave Hezekiah a choice in how to affirm his answer reveals the depth of their relationship. He honored Hezekiah's choice. What a mighty God we serve!

CHAPTER 4
Enoch

Enoch's life is a study in how to go hard after the heart of God, which is the central theme of both this book and the very existence of every dedicated saint of God. To understand what happened to Enoch we need to know what it takes to walk with God. In Amos 3:3: we read this: "Can two walk together, unless they are agreed?"

The first thing that is necessary in order to walk with God is to agree with God. That means you have accepted everything that God says to be truth, and are walking in agreement not only with God, but also with the words that He speaks. However, walking with God as Enoch did indicates a companionship—true and unadulterated relationship with God.

Secondly, part of walking with God indicates an involvement in each other's lives. On the part of humans, it would indicate a willingness to make God a part of each moment of life, and because we agree with Him, to please Him in everything we do and speak. That takes dying to self so that we can please God and it also takes dying to the world. This prevents distractions from your walk with God. This last part—communion with God—is very difficult for people to do on a consistent basis. However, it was apparently not as difficult for Enoch. This walk Enoch had did not begin until after the birth of Methuselah and continued for the next three hundred years.

The supporting scripture is Genesis 5:21-24: "Enoch lived sixty-five years and begot Methuselah. After he begat Methuselah, he walked with God three hundred years, and had sons and daughters. So all the days of Enoch were three hundred sixty-five years. And Enoch walked with God; and he was not for God took Him."

Who was Enoch? Adam begat Seth, Seth begat Enosh, Enosh begat Cainan, Cainan begat Mahalalel, Mahalalel begat Jared and Jared begat Enoch and Enoch begat Methuselah. Enoch was a descendant of Seth, the son of Adam, and the first man created as who was known to be godly in the line of Seth.

Enoch walked with God by putting his faith in Almighty God.
This very fact set him apart from others.

Let's find out what Enoch did before he was translated. The first thing he did was to walk with God. It was by faith that Enoch walked with God and Hebrews tells us that it is impossible to please God without faith, so this was an important path that Enoch intentionally sought.

The Greek translation of the Hebrew Bible renders this expression "Enoch pleased God," and this rendering was adopted by the writer of Hebrews. It is written in Hebrews

11:5-6: "By faith Enoch was taken away so that he did not see death, and was not found, because God had taken him; for before he was taken he had this testimony, that he pleased God. But without faith it is impossible to please Him, for he who comes to God must believe that He is, and that He is a rewarder of those who diligently seek Him."

This language seems to express the character and conduct of a man known for his love and devotion to God. Having been listed in this historical narrative; he must have been a man who lived an astonishing life, that he should have been singled out in this way for such a biography. There is no question that Enoch entered a more profound realization of the divine. He must have lived more in the realm of the eternal than did his contemporaries. Men looked at him and felt that there was an essence of God in him. Deep down in his soul there was a consciousness of God that they did not possess. Therefore, he stood out as a giant among his contemporaries.

Enoch was always pleasing to God, because he believed and lived in the power of his faith. His faith-filled walk resulted in great fellowship with God. This fellowship with God was his secret source of all that was great and wonderful in his life. He lived in a wicked time, in an age that was very corrupt, and yet during the wickedness that surrounded him, he lived a pure life before God and man. He was a man with ordinary passions and no doubt experienced failure and the normal distractions of life. However, the whole focus of his life was summed up in these words, "He walked with God."

Enoch and God had great companionship because they were two that walked together in agreement. To produce fellowship of this kind, there must be a unity of purpose and a harmony of oneness. These words imply a consistent, unbroken, communion with God. Enoch had risen above the shadows, idols, and pretenses, and with simple faith had grasped the unseen substance and reality of a personal God, his Father.

Enoch learned how to commune with God; his great faith in God caused him to have a pure walk with his Father. This why he pleased God. Enoch's faith made him trustworthy for God to spend time with him. It brought about a human-to-God that few had ever known. Time well spent with God alone brought this depth of knowing Him and continually seeking His presence in every moment of his life so far as it is possible for a human being to do so.

Enoch was taken by God, he was translated and did not see death. Genesis 5:24: reminds us: "And Enoch walked with God; and he was not, for God took him." Enoch left quietly; however, the people knew that God had taken him. He lived a relatively short life, but he was blessed in that he did not live to see the great corruption of the earth. He was translated before the flood.

Only one other person on earth was translated and that was the great prophet, Elijah. Elijah's departure from earth was a glorious event. We read this account in

2 Kings 2:11-13:

Then it happened, as they continued on and talked, then suddenly a chariot of fire appeared with horses of fire and separated the two of them; and Elijah went up by a whirlwind into heaven. And Elisha saw it, and he cried out, 'My father, my father, the chariot of Israel and its horsemen!' So he saw him no more. And he took hold of his own clothes and tore them into two pieces. He also took up the mantle of Elijah that had fallen from him and went back and stood by the bank of Jordan.

These are the only two people who are recorded in the Bible that were translated. It is interesting to note that Enoch left quietly with God; however, Elijah left suddenly in a chariot of fire drawn by horses of fire.

It seems to me that each man had a different ministry on earth, and they left this earth in a manner that mirrored their personalities. God is so good in that He loves us individually and responds to us in the way that we understand. He is a wonderful, loving Father.

Let us read in Hebrews 9:27: "And as it is appointed for men to die once, but after this the judgment." How do we reconcile this fact?

These two men are the only people in the Bible who did not see death. They will return as the two witnesses during the tribulation. Elijah is named as one of them and I believe that Enoch is the other one. Enoch did not see death and he also was the first prophet to announce the second coming of the LORD Jesus Christ as recorded in Jude 1:14-15 "Now Enoch, the seventh from Adam, prophesied about these men also, saying, 'Behold, the LORD comes with ten thousands of His saints, to execute judgment on all their ungodly deeds which they have committed in an ungodly way, and of all the harsh things which ungodly sinners have spoken against Him.'"

Zechariah, Malachi and John wrote about the two witnesses in the following scriptures.

Zechariah 4:11-14:

"Then I answered and said to him, 'What are these two olive trees—at the right of the lampstand and at its left?' And I further answered and said to him, 'What are these two olive branches that drip into the receptacles of the two golden pipes from which the golden oil drains?" Then he answered me and said, "Do you not know what these are?" And I said, "No, My LORD." "So he said "These are the two anointed ones, who stand beside the LORD of the whole earth."

Malachi 4:4-6:

Remember the Law of Moses, My servant, which I commanded him in Horeb for all Israel, with the statutes and judgments. Behold, I will send you Elijah the prophet before the coming of the great and dreadful day of the LORD. And he will turn the hearts of the fathers to the children, and the hearts of the children to their fathers, lest I come and strike the earth with a curse.

Revelation 11:3-12:

And I give power to my two witnesses, and they will prophesy one thousand two hundred and sixty days clothed in sackcloth. These are the two olive trees and the two lampstands standing before the God of the earth. And if anyone wants to harm them, fire proceeds from their mouth and devours their enemies. And if anyone wants to harm them, he must be killed in this manner. These have power to shut heaven, so that no rain falls in the days of their prophecy; and they have power over waters to turn them to blood, and to strike the earth with all plagues, as often as they desire. When they finish their testimony, the beast that ascends out of the bottomless pit will make war against them, overcome them and kill them. And their dead bodies will lie in the street of the great city which is spiritually is called Sodom and Egypt, where also our LORD was crucified. Then those from the peoples, tribes, tongues, and nations will see their dead bodies three-and-a-half days, and not allow their bodies to be put into graves. And those who dwell on the earth will rejoice over them, make merry, and send gifts to one another, because these two prophets tormented those who dwell on the earth. Now after the three-and-a-half days the breath of life from God entered them, and they stood on their feet, and great fear fell on those who saw them. And they heard a loud voice from heaven saying to the "Come up here." And they ascended to heaven in a cloud, and their enemies saw them.

This was their final departure to heaven. Elijah is named in the Bible as one of the Two Witnesses. It is my humble belief that Enoch is the other witness. He was a God seeker extraordinaire and he did not see death.

CHAPTER 5
Thirsting for God

David was not only a great warrior, he was also a great prayer warrior. He wrote many psalms of praise to God, and many prayers of pleading with God. As a result, he had a great relationship with his Father. In Psalm 46:10-11 he wrote "Be still and know that I am God; I will be exalted among the nations, I will be exalted in the earth! The LORD of hosts is with us: the God of Jacob is our refuge. Selah"

This is a commandment of God. This is the ultimate purpose for humankind on the earth. We must remove the roar of the earth so that we can hear His still small voice, the only powerful voice. We need to pray for God to enhance our listening ability.

We also need to slow down and sit before the LORD to marinate in His holy presence. These are the times we will remember, as they are precious to us, and they are also precious to Him. He waits for us, He longs for us, as a deer that pants after water, so does our God long for us. These are the times that we must record what He speaks to us; if we wait too long, we will miss the power of His words. If we do not record quickly, we may miss the exact words He spoke. This is very important.

He reminds us of Psalm 46:11 "The LORD of hosts is with us; the God of Jacob is our refuge. Selah" What does the LORD of hosts mean? It means Adonai Tzva - one of the names of God used approximately 235 times in the Bible. The literal meaning in Hebrew of Adonai is "The LORD of the Armies." Tzva is the word for army, and it references the Israeli Defense Force.

The Roman army had 5,000 men in a legion, and this remained so until the middle of the first century; however, God's army was a little different.

The LORD (Yahweh) of Armies—God's army—fights for us. At the time of the New Testament a legion of men was ideally 6,000 men and was divided into 10 cohorts of six hundred men each. They were further divided into "centuries" or Divisions of one hundred. A centurion was a position often mentioned in the New Testament, known as the officer in charge of one hundred men.

David urges us to be spiritually aware of the fact that God's army is with us and that He is our refuge. This is a powerful revelation, and we should never be afraid of any situation or circumstance as we mediate on the power that goes with us. This power—His—power, will keep us in His care. What a wonderful, powerful, loving Father we have! We must thank Him and praise Him for always being with us everywhere we go. We can feel safe knowing that His loving hand of protection is guiding us.

In Psalm 42:1–2 David writes "As the deer pants for the water brooks, so pants my soul for You, O God, My soul thirsts for God, for the living God. When shall I come and appear before God?"

The deer is found feeding near the water. When hunted he will take to the river, stay submerged as long as his breath permits, then swim downstream in the middle so as not to touch the branches of the trees on either side. This prevents the hounds from finding his scent. Sometimes he will stay in the water submerged with only his nose out, until he is chased. After being chased he becomes faint and longs for water. God is often pictured as the source of Living Water to satisfy our spiritual thirst.

This is not the quiet longing of inward desire, but the audible panting produced by the deer. This is an example of our great yearning for our God in the time of our distress; when this yearning is so deep, we physically feel it and cry aloud to our Father. We may also cry from deep within our soul and pray to God for relief. When this occurs, we are assured of His presence.

The following scriptures tell us what to thirst for:

Psalm 63:1:

"O God, You are my God; early will I seek You; My soul thirsts for You, My flesh longs for You, in a dry and thirsty land where there is no water." (This is thirsting for the living God.)

John 4:13-14:

"Jesus answered and said to her, 'Whoever drinks of this water will thirst again, but whoever drinks of the water that I shall give him *will never thirst.* But the water that I shall give him will become in him a fountain of water springing up into everlasting life." (Thirsting for salvation.)

Matthew 5:6:

"Blessed are those who hunger and thirst for righteousness, for they shall be filled." (Thirsting for right living.)

Proverbs 3:13-18:

"Happy is the man who finds wisdom, and the man who gains understanding; for her proceeds are better than the profits of silver, and her gain than fine gold. She is more precious than rubies, and all the things you may desire cannot compare with her. Length of days is in her right hand, in her left hand riches and honor. Her ways are ways of pleasantness, and all her paths are peace. She is a tree of life to those who take hold of her, and happy are all who retain her."

Proverbs 9:9-10:

"Give instruction to the wise man, and he will be still wiser; teach a just man, and he will increase in learning. The fear of the LORD is the beginning of wisdom, and the knowledge of the Holy One is understanding."

What powerful scriptures that challenge us to seek wisdom and knowledge! The promises of God are encouraging, and we know that the beginning of wisdom is knowing God.

Solomon was a very wise man and encourages us today to respect and seek wisdom from God. Wisdom and knowledge bring understanding.

In James 1:5 we read "If any of you lacks wisdom, let him ask of God, who gives to all liberally and without reproach, and it will be given to him."

God promises to give us wisdom if we ask Him for it. He says through Solomon that wisdom and knowledge of God is understanding and, regarding wisdom, He promises in Proverbs 9:11: "your days will be multiplied, and years of life will be added to you."

God clearly recognizes wisdom, knowledge and understanding as being important. He tells us how to obtain them and walk in them. It is no wonder that when He was on earth in human form that He was the master teacher. Praise His holy name! If we walk in ignorance, it is our decision because God has given us these great plans and promises.

John 7:37-39: "On the last day, that great day of the feast, Jesus stood and cried out, saying, 'If anyone thirsts, let him come to Me and drink. He who believes in Me, as the Scripture has said, out of his heart will flow rivers of living water.' But this He spoke concerning the Spirit, whom those believing in Him would receive; for the Holy Spirit was not yet given, because Jesus was not yet glorified."

All of this brings us to understand that thirst for more of God is what He desires. What does this do first? It enhances a knowledge of the power of God as a force to protect and defend us. When we know that the battle belongs to the LORD, it makes it easy to rest in His arms, saturated with His presence. We can trust Him wholly for He is holy.

Have you ever wondered why the title "LORD of Hosts" appears more frequently in the book of Malachi than any other book in the Old Testament? Could it be because, during the time of Isaiah, the Northern Kingdom was overrun and destroyed, and the Southern Kingdom was almost destroyed by the "Hosts" (armies) of Assyria? God's people had so few tools that the Assyrian King Sennacherib could mockingly challenge King Hezekiah with the offer of a gift of 2,000 horses 'if Hezekiah could find enough soldiers to ride them.' This was King Sennacherib's attempt at sarcastic humor.

Great thirst for God makes winning battles for the LORD much easier as we will read in the following scriptures. Great miracles followed these Israelite warriors because of prayer.

Isaiah 36:8: "Now therefore, I urge you, give a pledge to my master the king of Assyria, and I will give you two thousand horses—if you are able on your part to put riders on them!" The end of this battle was not good for King Sennacherib.

We find a similar situation in the period of Jeremiah. The Southern Kingdom was wiped out by the "HOSTS" (armies) of Babylon. This is found in Jeremiah 39:1: "In the ninth year of Zedekiah, king of Judah, in the tenth month, Nebuchadnezzar, king of Babylon, and all his army came against Jerusalem, and besieged it" Thus the fall of Jerusalem!

In the post exilic period of Malachi was the very small land of Judah, a tiny province, within the vast Persian Empire. Judah had no army of its own. It was precisely in such times that God's people were painfully aware of how limited their own resources were. There was great comfort in the fact that the LORD had His invincible heavenly armies ready to fight for His people.

It is like the comfort felt when Elisha prayed for his servant at Dothan when they were surrounded by the Syrian armies. It is written in 2 Kings 6:17: "And Elisha prayed and said, 'LORD, I pray, open his eyes that he may see.' Then the LORD opened the eyes of the young man, and he saw. And behold, the mountain was full of horses and chariots of fire all around Elisha."

This story is just too rich to discuss it only in a single verse. So, we will study

2 Kings 6:8-16, and see what a sense of humor God has. It will build our faith and encourage us to expect and see great things from our Father God.

The blinded Syrians were captured. In 2 Kings 6:8-16 we read:

Now the king of Syria was making war against Israel; and he consulted with his servants, saying, 'My camp will be in such and such a place.' And the man of God sent to the king of Israel, saying, 'Beware that you do not pass this place, for the Syrians are going down there.' Then the king of Israel sent someone to the place of which the man of God had told him. Thus he warned him, and he was watchful there, not just once or twice. Therefore the heart of the king of Syria was greatly troubled by this thing; and he called his servants and said to them, 'Will you not show me which of us is for the king of Israel?' And one of his servants said, 'None, my lord, O king; but Elisha, the prophet who is in Israel, tells the king of Israel the words that you speak in your bedroom.' So he said, 'Go and see where he is, that I may send and get him.' And it was told him, saying, 'Surely he is in Dothan.' Therefore he sent horses and chariots and a great army there, and they came by night and surrounded the city. And when the servant of the man of God arose early and went out, there was an army, surrounding the city with horses and chariots. And his servant said to him, 'Alas, my master! What shall we do?' So he answered, *'Do not fear, for those who are with us are more than those who are with them.'"*

We already know that Elisha prayed that He would open his servant's eyes so that he could see. God did open his eyes and he also gave him the gift of seeing the invisible armies that surrounded the city. That is our great Father who answers our prayers.

2 Kings 6:18-23:

"So when the Syrians came down to him, Elisha prayed to the LORD, and said, 'Strike this people, I pray with blindness.' And He struck them with blindness according to the word of Elisha. Now Elisha said to them, 'This is not the way, nor is this the city. Follow me, and I will bring you to the man whom you seek.' But he led them to Samaria. So it was, when they had come to Samaria, that Elisha said, 'LORD, open the eyes of these men, that they may see.' And the LORD opened their eyes, and they saw; and there they were, inside Samaria! Now when the king of Israel saw them, he said to Elisha, "My father, shall I kill them? Shall I kill them?' But he answered, 'You shall not kill them. Would you kill those whom you have taken captive with your sword and your bow? Set food and water before them, that they may eat and drink and go to their master.' Then he prepared a great feast for them; and after they ate and drank, he sent them away and they went to their master. So the bands of Syrian raiders came no more into *the land of* Israel."

Prayer opened the way to astounding victory!!

New Testament Affirmation of God's Protection through Legions of Angels:

Matthew 26:51-53: "And suddenly, one of those who were with Jesus stretched out his hand and drew his sword, struck the servant of the high priest and cut off his ear. But Jesus said to him, 'Put your sword in its place, for all who take the sword will perish by the sword. Or do you think that I cannot pray to My Father, and He will provide Me with more than twelve legions of angels." Twelve legions would be 72,000 angels.

How do we get to a spiritual level that we can commune with God, get answers and be sure that we have heard from Him? Yes, you can hear and believe God. It is accomplished with a great thirst for more of God, as well as spending time on your knees in prayer, Bible study, and fellowship with the saints. Let's explore what the scripture says about thirsting.

What the Scripture Says about Thirsting:

Spiritual thirst:

- Psalm 42:2: "My soul thirsts for God, for the living God: When shall come and appear before God?"
- Psalm 63:1 "O God, You are my God; early will I seek You; my soul thirsts for You; my flesh longs for You in a dry and thirsty land where there is no water."

- Psalm 143:6: "I spread out my hands to You; my soul longs for You like a thirsty land. Selah"
- Amos 8:11: "'Behold the days are coming,' says the LORD God, 'that I will send a famine on the land, not a famine of bread, nor a thirst for water, but of hearing the words of the LORD.'"

Living Water:

- Song of Solomon 4:15: (To the Beloved) "A fountain of gardens, a well of living waters, and streams from Lebanon."

  These are mountain streams from Lebanon. One could view the entire Promised Land from Lebanon's highest mountain peaks.

- Isaiah 49:10: "They shall neither hunger nor thirst, neither heat nor sun shall strike them; for He who has mercy on them will lead them, even by the springs of water He will guide them."

  God promises merciful protected guidance and food along the way.

- Isaiah: 55:1: "Ho! everyone who thirsts, come to the waters; and you, who have no money, come, buy and eat, yes, come buy wine and milk without money and without price."

This is an invitation to abundant life.

- Jeremiah. 17:13: "Thus says the LORD: 'O LORD, the hope of Israel, all who forsake You shall be ashamed. Those who depart from Me shall be written in the earth, because they have forsaken the LORD, the fountain of living waters.'" This is a call to eternal life in Christ.

Water issuing from God's house:

Ezekiel. 47:1: "Then he brought me back to the door of the temple; and there was water, flowing from under the threshold of the temple toward the east: for the front of the temple faced east and the water was flowing from under the right side of the temple, at the south of the altar." These are healing waters.

Joel 3:18: "And it will come to pass in that day that the mountains shall drip with new wine, the hills shall flow with milk, and all the brooks of Judah shall be flooded with water; a fountain shall flow from the house of the LORD and water the Valley of Acacias.'" This is God's blessing on His church.

Zechariah 14:8: "And in that day it shall be that living waters shall flow from Jerusalem, half of them toward the eastern sea and half of them toward the western sea; in both summer and winter it shall occur." This is the day of the LORD when fresh flowing, living waters will flow year-round from Jerusalem.

Christ is the Source:

John 4:10: **"Jesus** answered and said to her, 'If you knew the gift of God, and who it is who says to you, Give Me a drink, you would have asked Him, and He would have given you living water.'" Salvation is free and Jesus' living water is satisfying to the soul.

Living water satisfies the deepest needs:

John 7:37-38: "On the last day, that great day of the feast, Jesus stood and cried out, saying, 'If anyone thirsts let him come to Me and drink. He who believes in Me, as the Scripture has said, out of his heart will flow rivers of living water.'"

Jesus was the fulfillment of all that this ceremony represented.

The supply is inexhaustible:

Revelation 7:17: "For the Lamb who is in the midst of the throne will shepherd them and lead them to living fountains of waters. And God will wipe away every tear from their eyes."

The Lamb is the shepherd, Jesus Christ.

Makes life fruitful:

Revelation 22:1-2: "And he showed me a pure river of water of life, clear as crystal, proceeding from the throne of God and of the Lamb. In the middle of its street, and on either side of the river, was the tree of life, which bore twelve fruits, each tree yielding its fruit every month. The leaves of the tree were for the healing of the nations."

The river reminds us of blessings from God. The tree of life symbolizes abundant life which provides life and sustains health.

Universal call to partake:

Revelation 22:17: "And the Spirit and the bride say, 'Come!' And let him who hears say, 'Come!' And let him who thirsts come. Whoever desires, let him take the water of life freely."

Those who are thirsting will come to the water of life.

Other descriptions of Living Water:

- A **B**rook—Psalm 110:7: "He shall drink of the brook by the wayside; therefore He shall lift up the head." This is David referring to the fact that, after the battle, he is refreshed as if he were drinking from a cool brook.

- A **W**ell—Isaiah. 12:3: 'Therefore with joy you will draw water from the wells of salvation." God's well is salvation and it will always bring great joy.

- A **F**ountain—Jeremiah 2:13: "For My people have committed two evils: they have forsaken Me, the fountain of living waters, and hewn themselves cisterns—broken cisterns that can hold no water."

God's people had forsaken Him, the living waters, and had turned to broken cisterns who were made by men and leaked. The two evils were forsaking God and replacing Him.

- A **Ri**ver—Ezekiel 47:5: "Again he measured one-thousand, and it was a river that I could not cross; for the water was too deep, water in which one must swim, a river that could not be crossed." As New Testament believers we have two golden opportunities available to us. By faith we can expect to see the heavenly temple from whence flows the river of God. This river brings life and healing to everything it touches. We can walk in that river of God now through the power of the Holy Spirit and God's resurrection power in us. Our Father God wants us to bring wholeness to everything we touch; and He makes this possible as His power flows through us.

Spiritual thirst is satisfied:

- Psalm 36:8-9: "They are abundantly satisfied with the fullness of Your house, and You give them drink from the river of Your pleasures. For with You is the fountain of life; in Your light we see light."
- Isaiah 44:3: "For I will pour water on him who is thirsty, and floods on the dry ground; I will pour My spirit on your descendants, and My blessing on your offspring;"

- Matthew 5:6: "Blessed are those who hunger and thirst for righteousness, for they shall be filled."
- John 6:35: "And Jesus said to them, 'I am the bread of life. He who comes to Me shall *never hunger*, and he who believes in Me shall *never thirst*.'"
- Revelation 22:17: "And the Spirit and the bride say, "Come!" And let him who hears says 'Come!' And let him who thirsts come. Whoever desires, let him take the water of life freely."
- Revelation 21:6-7: "And He said to me, 'It is done! I am the Alpha and the Omega, the Beginning and the End. I will give of the fountain of the water of life freely to him who thirsts. He who overcomes shall inherit all things, and I will be his God and he shall be My son.'"

Spiritual fullness satisfies the deepest needs of the soul:

- Psalm 23:5: "You prepare a table before me in the presence of my enemies: You anoint my head with oil; my *cup runs over*."
- Malachi 3:10: "Bring all the tithes into the storehouse, that there may be food in My house, and try Me now in this, says the LORD of hosts, 'If I will not open for you the windows of heaven and pour out for you such *blessing* that there will not be room enough to receive it.'"
- John 15:11: (Jesus speaking) "'These things I have spoken to you, that My joy may remain in you and that your joy may be *full*.'"

- Romans 15:29: "But I know that when I come to you, I shall come in the *fullness* of the blessing of the gospel of Christ."
- Ephesians 3:19: "To know the love of Christ which passes knowledge; that you may be filled with all the *fullness* of God."
- Ephesians 5:18 "And do not be drunk with wine, in which is dissipation, but be *filled* with the Spirit."

Fullness of wisdom is found in Christ:

Colossians 1:19: "For it pleased the *Father* that in *Him* all the fullness should dwell."

When Christ Lives in Us, We Have *ALL* We Need:

The battle truly is the LORD's. However, we can arm ourselves through seeking God. Prayer can be times of refreshment, times of healing, times of deliverance and more importantly times that deepen our thirst for more of God and less of us.

.

"Enoch walked with God; and he was not, for God took him." (Genesis 5:24). Let this be the prayer of our heart. Then and only then, can we be victorious through Christ when the battle comes. We will be prepared, and God will prevail for us. "If God be for us who can be against us" Romans 8:31. *No one!*

Elijah, the great prophet, drew down fire from heaven, healed the sick, raised the dead, delivered Israel from pagan worship, parted the River Jordan and walked with God. He went to heaven in a whirlwind riding in a chariot of fire drawn by horses of fire especially designed by his Father God. Elijah was a prayer warrior, and he had an intimate relationship with God. He spoke to Him in prayer like a son would to his daddy, however, this Father was the great God of the Universe. His prayer life is what enabled him to minister in the power of God.

Enoch and Elijah were the only men in the Bible who did not see death. Both were translated. All the heroes of the faith had one thing in common: they had a continual thirst for more of God.

CHAPTER 6
Waiting for God

There are many scriptures that contain various forms of the word WAIT and show the importance that God places on the time we wait on Him, and Him alone. He is the only source of wisdom, knowledge and understanding. To know Him is to wait on Him and listen to Him. The very fact that many scriptures contain the word WAIT tells us repeatedly just how much our presence means to our Father. There are approximately forty verses in the Bible that speak about "waiting" for God."

Simeon, Anna, and David: Prayer Warriors Who Waited on God

Simeon, The Man in the Temple

Who was the man called Simeon? He must have been important as the great artist Rembrandt painted him several times to commemorate Simeon with the baby Jesus in the temple, when he sang what is known as "Simeon's Song," and when he prophesied to Mary about Jesus. These paintings were seen in the early seventeenth century. This speaks to the reverence that the Christian church had for the birth of Jesus Christ and the great men in the Bible.

Simeon was a resident of Jerusalem, and like the whole of Israel, was waiting for Jesus, the consolation, to come. He was a godly man who was longing for the birth of Jesus. It might also be noted that, his name means "God-Receiver." And that is exactly what he did in receiving the Messiah in the temple. What an awesome moment that must have been for him! To be chosen to literally be a "God-Receiver." I feel as though this is a high and holy moment to even write this. Can you begin to imagine how heavy the anointing of God had to be on him at that moment? It was a very reverent encounter. This awesome event was recorded in God's word.

Let us begin with Jesus being presented in the temple. In Luke 2:22-24 we read "Now when the days of her purification according to the law of Moses were completed, they brought Him to Jerusalem to present Him to the LORD. (as it is written in the law of the Lord, 'Every male who opens the womb shall be called holy to the LORD'), and to offer a sacrifice according to what is said in the law of the LORD, 'A pair of turtledoves or two young pigeons.'" In the Old Testament we read: "Then the LORD spoke to Moses, saying, "Consecrate to Me all the firstborn, whatever opens the womb among the children of Israel, both of men and beast; it is Mine'"(Exodus 13:1-2).

Simeon was a righteous, devout man who was eagerly waiting for the Messiah to come and rescue Israel. The Holy Spirit was upon him and had revealed to him that he would not die until he had seen the LORD's Messiah. On a certain day the Spirit led him to the temple. When Mary and Joseph entered the temple to present the baby Jesus, Simeon was there. The temple had many doors, and it was a divine appointment that the holy family entered the door close to where Simeon was standing. "He took Him up in his arms and blessed God, and said: 'LORD now You are letting Your servant depart in peace, according to Your word; for my eyes have seen Your salvation, which you have prepared before the face of all peoples, a light to bring revelation to the Gentiles, and the glory of Your people Israel (Luke 2:29-32).'" This is known as Simeon's Song.

Jesus' parents were amazed at what was being said about him. "Then Simeon blessed them, and he prophesied to Mary, His mother, 'Behold this Child is destined for the fall and rising of many in Israel, and for a sign which will be spoken against (yes, a sword will pierce through your own soul also), that the thoughts of many hearts may be revealed'" (Luke 2:34-35).

This passage indicates that Jesus would reveal the truth and be accepted as the consolation of Israel by *some* of the Jews. There would be opposition and his suffering would cause great personal pain to Mary. That sword would pierce her broken heart.

Simeon spent his life anticipating Christ's arrival as we, in a similar way, should live our lives waiting for his return.

Acts 1:10-11: "And while they looked steadfastly toward heaven as He went up, behold, two men stood by them in white apparel, who also said, 'Men of Galilee, why do you stand gazing up into heaven? This same Jesus, who was taken up from you into heaven, will so come in like manner as you saw Him go into heaven.'"

Titus 2:13: "Looking for the blessed hope and glorious appearing of our great God and Savior Jesus Christ." This was Paul instructing Titus on the qualities of a sound church. It was important for them to understand grace. They were to have great hope in Jesus, and to look for His glorious return.

Anna, a Great Woman of God

Anna appears in the listing of the thirty-six prayer warriors recorded as having fasted and prayed. However, let us focus on how long she waited to see her Savior. She waited in the temple.

Rembrandt painted Anna as a pious prophetess whose advanced age and honorable behavior ushered in the new covenant. He also painted Simeon and Anna with baby Jesus. Anna arrives at the purification of Mary, with Joseph and Jesus in the temple, forty days after Jesus' birth. It is a scene repeated over and over in Israelite culture, for the law required a sacrifice. Anna has three short verses in the Bible that vividly depicted her as a woman deserving the honor bestowed on the elderly in the ancient Mediterranean world. She is the New Testament's only named female prophetess. Luke tells us her father's name was Phanuel. He also mentioned that she is from the tribe of Asher. As such, she numbers among the few New Testament characters with tribal listings.

In Deuteronomy 33:24-25 we read "And of Asher he said: 'Asher is most blessed of sons; let him be favored by his brothers and let him dip his foot in oil. Your sandals shall be iron and bronze; as your days so shall your strength be.'"

The tribe of Asher was promised great strength all the days of their lives. They also had beautiful and talented women in their tribe. These gifts qualified them for royal and high priestly marriages. Anna was a strong woman for all those years. She lived in the temple, some say in a room, some say in an apartment. We know that wherever she lived she prayed day and night. We also know that the singers of the Levites lived in the chambers in the temple as we read in I Chronicles 9:33: "These are the singers, heads of the fathers' houses of the Levites, who lodged in the chambers, and were free from other duties; for they were employed in that work day and night."

As a prophetess Anna received insight into things that normally remain hidden to ordinary people. She recognized who this child was and told of His significance to the people who had been waiting for the Messiah and were near the temple on this special day. Her actions affirm Amos 3:7:

"Surely the LORD God does nothing, unless He reveals His secret to His servants the prophets."

As I have previously discussed, the three verses in the Bible written about Anna are Luke 2:36-38: "Now there was one, Anna, a prophetess, the daughter of Phanuel, of the tribe of Asher. She was of a great age and had lived with a husband seven years from her virginity; and this woman was a widow of about eighty-four years, who did not depart from the temple, but served God with fastings and prayers, night and day. And coming in that instant she gave thanks to the LORD and spoke of Him to all those who looked for redemption in Jerusalem."

In review, Anna was a prophetess, of great age. How encouraging it is to meet those who, through a long life, have remained true to the LORD, whose gray hairs are honorable because of a life lived in His divine will. When they die, they are ready for the glory of heaven. She was a widow. God withdrew from her the earthly love she rejoiced in; however, she did not bury her hope in her husband's grave. In the place of what God took, He gave her more of Himself. She became devoted to Him who had promised to be the husband to the widow, and through her long widowhood was unwavering in her devotion to Him. Anna did not depart from the temple attending the night and day services of the temple.

In Proverbs 16:31 we read: "The silver-haired head is a crown of glory, if it is found in the way of righteousness." She trusted in God and her silver head was a crown of glory.

Her seat in the temple was always occupied. She served the LORD with many fastings. Without a doubt, Anna was one of God's own elect. She was willing to miss a meal in order to spend more time before God. Her life was one of godly self-control. She had learned how to crucify the flesh in order to serve God more acceptably. She gave thanks unto the LORD and the fact that she was in the temple when Jesus came with his parents was no coincidence. It was a day that she had long prayed for. When she entered the temple that day, she heard sounds of exultation and joy proceeding from the inner court, and then from the lips of Simeon she heard these words in Luke 2:29-30: "LORD, now, You are letting Your servant depart in peace, according to Your word; for my eyes have seen Your salvation." Anna knew her time had come to see the Messiah face to face.

In Luke 2:38: We remember that she "spoke of Him to all." She then became an evangelist and went out into Jerusalem to proclaim the Messiah is here. He is in the temple. Rejoice for our salvation is at hand. She waited to see Jesus and her prayers were answered.

What a wonderful life she lived. Anna had reason to feel sorry for herself, her husband died young, and she had no children. However, she lived her life with peace and joy in the temple seeking God. She did not look back, she looked to the future with hope. She was a prayer warrior, and her greatest prayer was answered. Her focus was on the future, looking for the Messiah.

Her world was very much a male-dominated one where women were expected to be silent and unobtrusive. Anna was God-focused. We must ask ourselves "What is our focus?"

David, a Great Writer

David wrote seventy-five of the one-hundred-fifty psalms written in the book of Psalms. He was a great musician and a wonderful writer of beautiful praises to God. David loved music and was known for being an accomplished lyrist. According to 1 Samuel 16:23, whenever King Saul had a distressing spirit, he called for David to come play the lyre for him. He would then become refreshed. The lyre is an ancient musical instrument that was played in the temple. David was well known for his musical talents and played many instruments; however, he was well known as an accomplished lyrist.

Waiting on God all day was one of David's secrets of being a man after God's own heart. I will list a few of his beautiful psalms revealing his great love for God and how his heart longed for God in those quiet times of waiting.

David, a Great King, Warrior, Musician

- Psalm 25:3: "Indeed, let no one who waits on You be ashamed; Let those be ashamed who deal treacherously without cause."

- Psalm 25:5: "Lead me in Your truth and teach me, for You are the God of my salvation; on You I wait all the day You."
- Psalm 25:21: "Let integrity and uprightness preserve, for I wait for You."
- Psalm 27:14: "Wait on the LORD; be of good courage, and He shall strengthen your heart; Wait, I say, on the LORD!"
- Psalm 33:20: "Our soul waits for the LORD; He is our help and our shield."
- Psalm 37:7: "Rest in the LORD and wait patiently for Him; do not fret because of him who prospers in his way, because of the man who brings wicked schemes to pass."
- Psalm 37:9: "For evil doers shall be cut off; but those who wait on the LORD, they shall inherit the earth."
- Psalm 37:34: "Wait on the LORD and keep His way, and He shall exalt you to inherit the land; when the wicked are cut off, you shall see it."
- Psalm 40:1: "I waited patiently for the LORD; and He inclined to me and heard my cry."
- Psalm: 52:9: "I will praise you forever, because You have done it; and in the presence of Your saints I will wait on Your name, for it is good."
- Psalm 59:9: "I will wait for You, O You his Strength; for God is my defense."
- Psalm 62:1,5: "Truly my soul silently waits for God; from Him comes my salvation." "My, soul, wait silently for God alone, for my expectation is from Him." In

these verses David is telling his soul to be quiet so he can hear God speak to Him.

- Psalm 69:6: "Let not those who wait for You, O Lord God of hosts, be ashamed because of me; let not those who seek You be confounded because of me, O God of Israel."
- Psalm 130:5-6: "I wait for the LORD, my soul *waits*, and in His word I do hope. My soul *waits* for the Lord more than those who watch for the morning— Yes, more than those who watch for the morning."

The Hebrew word *qavah* - means to bind together by twisting; (binding together, to tarry, to eagerly wait) as in waiting, like an extension cord from one point to another with the thought that God is at one end of the cord and the human heart at the other end pulling at God and longing for Him more than the last watch at night. The watchman is longing to be relieved of his duty at the coming of the day. The fact that this is repeated two times in this scripture emphasizes David's great longing for God.

Others Who Waited for the LORD

- Jacob—Genesis 49:18: "I have waited for your salvation, O LORD!"
- Isaiah—Isaiah 8:17: "And I will wait on the LORD, who hides His face from the house of Jacob; and I will hope in Him."

- Jeremiah—14:22: "Are there any among the idols of the nations that can cause rain? Or can the heavens give showers? Are You not He, O LORD our God? Therefore we will wait for You, since You have made all these."

- Micah—Micah 7:7: "Therefore, I will look to the LORD; I will wait for the God of my salvation; My God will hear me."

How to Wait for God

The first step is to exercise your faith, for in Hebrews 11:6 He tells us: "But without faith *it is* impossible to please *Him*, for he who comes to God must believe *that* He is, and that He is a rewarder of those who *diligently* seek Him." This enables us to come to God *expecting* to receive from Him. The more you pray, the more you get answers, and your faith grows. Prayer brings us into an intimate relationship with our Father. As you grow in this dimension your entire spiritual being is refreshed and you can hear His voice more clearly and discernment is also increased. Your eyes of understanding can see Him at work on your behalf.

You should choose a quiet place away from distractions of the world to be used as your prayer room. This becomes a place where you meet with God. He longs for your presence and to hear your voice. You will be excited to go to your meeting place and your *longing* for more of God will increase. When going to your secret place to pray, it is important to still your mind and mediate only on God, sending worldly thoughts and distractions out of your mind so that you approach God with a single mind and heart for Him. Sit quietly before God, meditate on His majesty, and prayers will flow from your heart.

It is important to wait *patiently* for Him, and to record what He says to you while you take time to *listen* for Him to speak. At other times you will just have an inner peace that passes all understanding and that may be all that He says. You will also experience overwhelming joy. He will speak to you in ways that He knows you will understand. God knows that His children are all different, and as a good Father, He speaks to us in a way that is best for us. We must earnestly and *continually* seek His face.

These are just a few scriptures that confirm how to wait for God:

- Lamentations 3:26: "It is good that one should hope and wait quietly for the salvation of the LORD."
- Hosea 12:6: "So you, by the help of your God, return; observe mercy and justice, and wait on your God *continually*."

Blessings from God for those Who Wait on Him

Isaiah 40:31: "But those who wait on the Lord shall renew their strength; they shall mount up with wings like eagles, they shall run and not be weary, they will walk and not faint." God promises you great strength so that you can soar like the eagles, run with abundant strength, and walk without fear of fainting. Our God is an awesome God.

Psalm 91:1: "He who dwells in the secret place of the Most High shall abide under the shadow of the Almighty." We have a bomb shelter made of feathers. God gives us great protection as He goes with us on our journey through the earth.

Lamentations 3:25: "The LORD is good to those who wait for Him, to the soul who seeks Him." Those who seek and wait for Him will enjoy the goodness of God.

Psalm. 40:1-3: "I waited patiently for the LORD; and He inclined to me and heard my cry. He also brought me up out of a horrible pit, out of the miry clay, and set my feet on upon a rock, and established my steps. He has put a new song in my mouth—praise to our God; many will see it and fear and will trust in the LORD." God will be gracious to us as He gives us mercy and justice. All who wait for Him are blessed. God is the best Father we could ever have. He knows our flaws and continues to love us. These are just a few of His blessings. The greatest one is that He gives Himself to us through Jesus Christ His only Son. We are a blessed people, the people of God.

CHAPTER 7
Hall of Faith

The entire chapter eleven of Hebrews is known as "The Hall of Faith" and is to be revered. The list of saints included gives us a snapshot of who truly sought God the way we want to, how they did it, and the glorious results.

Hebrews 11:6 "But without faith it is impossible to please Him, for he who comes to God must believe that He is and that He is a rewarder of those who diligently seek Him."

God's Seekers and God's Warriors

Hebrews 11:1-3

"Now faith is the substance of things hoped for, the evidence of things not seen. For by it the elders obtained a good testimony. By faith we understand that the worlds were framed by the word of God, so that the things which are seen were not made of things which are visible."

The following people are named in Hebrews 11:

- Abel presented an excellent sacrifice to God and therefore was known for his righteousness.
- Enoch pleased God and did not see death. He was taken by God, and it was remembered that he pleased Him. What a wonderful example of faith!
- Noah by faith prepared the ark for the saving of his household. He condemned the world and therefore was esteemed for his righteousness. Noah did not fear when God told him to build the ark, and the people ridiculed him. He had a very strong faith and was devoted to his calling.
- Sarah received strength to conceive and bore the child when she was well past the child-bearing age. She had a strong faith "because she judged Him faithful who had promised" (Hebrews 11:11).

Abraham by faith obeyed when called to go out to a place where he would have an inheritance. He went out not knowing where he was going. He literally defied his intellect, believing in a higher power who knows all things. He trusted in His call. Abraham was raised from the dead as he was past the age of giving seed to Sarah for Isaac to be born. He lived in temporary housing (tents) with Isaac and Jacob, his co-heirs of the same promise. God had prepared a place for them. They trusted Him as they sought the homeland. But now they desired a better home, a heavenly home. God says he is proud to be called their Father and has prepared a city for them.

- By faith Isaac blessed Jacob and Esau
- By faith Jacob, when dying, blessed each of the sons of Joseph while leaning on top of his staff.
- By faith, when Joseph was dying, he gave instruction saying, "'Take my bones and bury them with you when you depart for the promised land'" (Hebrews 11:22).
- Moses' parents hid him for three months; they were not afraid of the king's command. By faith Moses refused to be called the son of Pharoah's daughter, choosing to suffer with the people of God rather than to enjoy the pleasures of Egypt. He esteemed the approval of Christ greater than the treasures of Egypt; for he looked to the reward. By faith he left Egypt not fearing the king's wrath for he was led by the invisible hand of God. He endured as seeking Him who is invisible. He kept the Passover to save the first-born from death and led God's children through the Red Sea.
- The Egyptians attempted to cross the Red Sea and drowned.
- Rehab by faith did not die with those who did not believe because she had taken care of the spies to save their lives.
- "And what more shall I say? For the time would fail me to tell of Gideon and Barak; Samson and Jephthah, also of David, Samuel, and the prophets" (Hebrews 11:32).
- Unnamed heroes of the faith accomplished the following works of God's power through them:
  - Subdued kingdoms.
  - Worked righteousness.

- Obtained promises.
- Stopped the mouths of lions.
- Quenched the violence of fire.
- Escaped the edge of the sword.
- Out of weakness were made strong.
- Became valiant in battle.
- Turned the flights of the alien armies.
- Women saw their dead raised to life.
- Others were tortured, knowing they had a heavenly reward waiting for them.
- Many were chained and put in prison for years.
- There were Christians who were killed by the sword, suffered extreme poverty and other afflictions for their faith.
- These weary people "wandered in deserts and mountains, in dens and caves of the earth" (Hebrews 11:38).

Hebrews 11:39-40: "And all of these, having obtained a good testimony through faith, did not receive the promise (of going into the promised land). God having proved something better for us, that they would not be made perfect apart from us."

God's word reminds us that historic figures have encountered this Creator in personal ways, revealing that He is more than a force; He is a personal God who relates to those who seek Him in providential and redemptive ways. Those who are worthy approach God understanding that they must have faith as a starting point and realistic goals. Prayer and faith make this a reality. "For without faith it is impossible to please God" (Hebrews 11:6).

James 5:16: "The effective fervent prayer of a righteous man avails much."

Faith untested is simply mental assent.

CHAPTER 8
Elijah

These scriptures which we quoted earlier in the book in support of the power of prayer and fasting also serve to emphasize God's revelation to Elijah which resulted in a manifest presence of God.

Elijah was a prophet among all prophets. He appeared out of nowhere and left in a chariot of fire pulled by horses of fire. He will reappear before the second advent of Christ to evangelize the Jewish people. He was known as Elijah the Tishbite as he was from Tishbe. He was one of the greatest prophets of Jehovah and his background suited him to be the hand-picked servant of God at a time when the worship of Baal was rampant and in competition with the God of Israel. Elijah was the chosen vessel to make war against this pagan god. He deserves special attention because he was singularly devoted to God, sought Him with every ounce of his being, and lived an astounding faith-filled life as a result.

Living in Tishbe, in Gilead, which is a historical region east of the Jordan, prepared him for the task that God set before him. The inhabitants of the region were not civilized like those who formed the communities of Ephraim and Judah, but were wandering people, with irregular habits, exposed to the attacks of nomadic tribes of the desert. He appeared abruptly before the throne of Ahab. Elijah was known for his long, thick hair hanging down his back. This was reminiscent of Samson and the accompanying powers of endurance which he possessed. His clothing consisted of a girdle made of animal skin which he used to gird up his loins when he had to move quickly. His mantle was made of sheep or goat skin which he would roll up to make a staff or hold it over the Jordan River to part the waters. At times he covered his face with it; he also wore it as a cape.

Elijah had plenty of time to pray and listen to God all those years that he spent in the rugged land of Gilead. He dug a deep well with the Almighty God and that is one of the great attributes of Elijah. One of his legacies is that he accomplished these great miracles through the power of prayer. James 5:16-18 attests to this fact. "Confess your trespasses to one another, and pray for one another, that you may be healed. The effective fervent prayer of a righteous man avails much." Elijah was a man with a nature like ours, and he prayed earnestly that it would not rain; and it did not rain on the land for three years and six months. And he prayed again, and the heaven gave rain, and the earth produced fruit.

Elijah was a strong, bold prayer warrior. When he went to battle with Ahab he prayed. 1 Kings 18:36-38:

And it came to pass, at the time of the offering of the evening sacrifice, that Elijah the prophet came near and said, "LORD God of Abraham, Isaac, and Israel, let it be known this day that You are God in Israel and I am Your servant, and that I have done all these things at Your word. Hear me, O LORD, hear me, that this people may know that You are the LORD God, and that you have turned their hearts back to You again." Then the fire of the LORD fell and consumed the burnt sacrifice, and the wood and the stones and the dust, and it licked up the water that was in the trench.

This bold prayer got the attention of Ahab and even changed the weather patterns. This is important to know because Baal was very much a nature god and he was worshiped as such. So, for our God to take over his territory in a miracle must have had a great effect on the worshipers of Baal, diminishing his authority in the eyes of his people. The power of prayer through the prophet Elijah accomplished this. Without a doubt, He walked with God. He truly possessed holy boldness, always trusting God to accomplish His work through His people, the nation of Israel.

We also see Elijah on the Mount of Transfiguration talking with Jesus. What an honor this was as Moses and Elijah, representing the Law and the Prophets, appeared talking with Him. All those years of seeking God strengthened him for the work that God had called him to. Out of all the servants that God had, he chose Moses and Elijah to come to the Mount. They had sought Him and now He sought them. God is a great God, and He sees the heart of His seekers.

This occurred after Elijah's translation to heaven. Matthew recorded this in chapter 17:1-3: "Now after six days Jesus took Peter, James, and John his brother, led them up on a high mountain by themselves; and He was transfigured before them. His face shone like the sun, and His clothes became as white as the light. And behold, Moses and Elijah appeared to them, talking with Him."

Elijah will appear again at the second advent of Jesus Christ. He is one of the two witnesses who will evangelize the Jews in Israel. Malachi 4:5-6: "Behold, I will send you Elijah the prophet, before the coming of the great and dreadful day of the LORD. And he will turn the hearts of the fathers to their children, and the hearts of children to their fathers, lest I come, and strike the earth with a curse."

Little is known about Elijah other than his father was Sabach. God did not deem a history of Elijah necessary. He wanted us to see Him through Elijah. His spiritual parentage was more important in that he was a child of God who stood faithful to God during unfaithfulness. Elijah was willing to be faceless for others to see God in him. He did not care what people thought; he was true only to God his Father. He was single-minded and sought to do the will of God in perilous times. Israel was at a crisis point as there were so many pagan priests that even lived and ate in the king's palace. Jezebel, the king's wife, was a one-hundred-percent follower of Baal. She was a pagan to the highest degree and greatly influenced her husband.

So, we see Elijah was chosen to return God's people to Himself, and he set about to accomplish this very task. When it was completed, he left town in a chariot of fire with horses of fire and went up by a whirlwind into heaven. He appeared out of nowhere and left just as abruptly. His entire journey on earth seems to be expressly designed by his Father God. He was a good son who truly did his best to follow the leading of his Father.

Now let us study the heart of God's message through Elijah.

Elijah proclaimed a drought

We see him standing before King Ahab saying, in 1 Kings 17:1 "'As the LORD God of Israel lives, before whom I stand, there shall not be dew nor rain these years, except at my word.'" At this point God closed the heavens and they did not have rain for three-one-half years. In 1 Kings 16:33 we read "And Ahab made a wooden image. Ahab did more to provoke the LORD God of Israel to anger than all the kings of Israel who were before him."

Ahab shook his fist in the face of God, and his end was not good.

God then directed Elijah to leave and hide by the Brook Cherith, which flows into the Jordan. In 1 Kings 17:4-7: we read "'And it will be that you shall drink from the brook, and I have commanded the ravens to feed you there.' So he went and did according to the word of the LORD, for he stayed by the Brook Cherith, which flows into the Jordan. The ravens brought him bread and meat in the morning and bread and meat in the evening; and he drank from the brook. And it happened after a while that the brook dried up, because there had been no rain in the land."

Once again, the power of prayer in the life of Elijah was shown. His close relationship with God yielded such loving care from his Father.

Elijah and the widow

1 Kings. 17:8-14:

Then the word of the LORD came to him, saying, "Arise go to Zarephath, which belongs to Sidon, and dwell there. See, I have commanded a widow there to provide for you." So he arose and went to Zarephath. And when he came to the gate of the city, indeed a widow was there gathering sticks. And he called to her and said, "Please bring me a little water in a cup, that I may drink." And as she was going to get it, he called to her and said, "Please bring me a morsel of bread in your hand." So she said, "As the LORD your God lives, I do not have bread, only a handful of flour in a bin, and a little oil in a jar; and see, I am gathering a couple of sticks that I may go in and prepare it for myself and my son, that we may eat it, and die." And Elijah said to her, "Do not fear; go and do as you have said, but make me a small cake from it first, and bring it to me; and afterward make some for yourself and your son." For thus says the LORD God of Israel: "The bin of flour shall not be used up, nor shall the jar of oil run dry, until the day the LORD sends rain on the earth."

God was faithful to His word; the supply of flour and oil lasted many days. He was caring for His beloved Elijah. All those years of preparation in prayer was stored in the bank of Heaven and God honored them.

Elijah revived the widow's son

1 Kings 17:17-24:

Now it happened that the son of the woman who owned the house became sick. And his sickness was so serious that there was no breath left in him. So she said to Elijah, 'What have I to do with you, O man of God? Have you come to me to bring my sin to remembrance, and to kill my son?' And he said to her, 'Give me your son.' So he took him out of her arms and carried him to the upper room where he was staying, and laid him on his own bed. Then he cried out to the LORD said, 'O LORD my God, have You also brought tragedy on the widow with whom I lodge by killing her son?' And he stretched himself out on the child three times, and cried out to the LORD and said, 'O LORD my God, I pray, let this child's soul come back to him.' Then the LORD heard the voice of Elijah; and the soul of the child came to him, and he revived. And Elijah took the child and brought him down from the upper room into the house and gave him his mother. And Elijah said, 'See, your son lives!' Then the woman said to Elijah, 'Now by this I know that you are a man of God, and that the word of the LORD in your mouth is the truth.'" Elijah's prayers were effective because of his great intimacy with God.

Elijah's message to Ahab

We read in 1 Kings 18:1: "And it came to pass after many days that the word of the LORD came to Elijah, in the third year, saying. 'Go present yourself to Ahab, and I will send rain to the earth.'"

And we read in 1 Kings 18:3-4: "And Ahab had called Obadiah who was in charge of the house of Ahab. (Now, Obadiah feared the LORD greatly. For so it was while Jezebel massacred the prophets of the LORD, that Obadiah had taken one hundred prophets, fifty to each cave, and had fed them bread and water."

Ahab and Obadiah went into the land to look for springs of water and brooks in search of grass for the livestock. They divided the land to be searched; with Ahab going one way and Obadiah the other.

Now as Obadiah was on his way, suddenly Elijah met him; and he recognized him, and fell on his face, and said, 'Is that you, my lord, Elijah? 'And he answered, 'It is I. Go, tell your master that Elijah is here'" (1 Kings 18:7-8).

Obadiah became concerned for his safety.

1 Kings 18:9-12:

"So he said, 'How have I sinned, that you are delivering your servant into the hand of Ahab, to kill me? As the LORD your God lives, there is no nation or kingdom where my master has not sent someone to hunt for you; and when they said, 'He is not here,' he took an oath from the kingdom or nation that they could not find you. And now you say 'Go, tell your master that Elijah is here!'" And it shall come to pass, as soon as I am gone from you, that the Spirit of the LORD will carry you to a place I do not know; so when I go and tell Ahab, and he cannot find you, he will kill me. But I your servant have feared the LORD from my youth."

1 Kings 18:13-19

"Was it not reported to my lord what I did when Jezebel killed the prophets of the LORD, how I hid one hundred men of the LORD's prophets, fifty to a cave, and fed them with bread and water? And now you say, 'Go, tell your master, "Elijah is here." He will kill me!" Then Elijah said, "As the LORD of hosts lives, before whom I stand, I will surely present myself to him today." So Obadiah went to meet Ahab and told him; and Ahab went to meet Elijah. Then it happened, when Ahab saw Elijah, that Ahab said to him, 'Is that you, O troubler of Israel?' And he answered, "I have not troubled Israel, but you and your father's house have, in that you have forsaken the commandments of the LORD and have followed the Baals. Now therefore, send and gather all Israel to me on Mount

Carmel, the four-hundred-and-fifty prophets of Baal, and the four-hundred prophets of Asherah, who eat at Jezebel's table.'"

Miraculously, Ahab took the instruction of God through Elijah and did exactly as Elijah had told him to do. This miracle was the answer to Elijah's prayer. He had a plan that God had ordained, and this meeting had happened to bring it to pass. Elijah's intimacy with God led to authority in both the spiritual and physical realms.

Elijah's Mount Carmel victory

1 Kings 18:20-40:

So Ahab sent for all the children of Israel and gathered the prophets together on Mount Carmel. And Elijah came to all the people and said, 'How long will you falter between two opinions? If the LORD is God, follow Him; but if Baal, follow him.' But the people said not a word. Then Elijah said to the people, 'I alone am left a prophet of the LORD; but Baal's prophets are four hundred-and-fifty men. Therefore, let them give us two bulls; and let them choose one bull for themselves, cut in it pieces, and lay it on the wood, but put no fire under it, and I will prepare the other bull, and lay it on the wood, but put no fire under it. Then you call on the name of your gods, and I will call on the name of the LORD; and the God who answers by fire, He is God.' So all the people answered and said, 'It is well spoken.' Now Elijah said to the prophets of Baal, 'Choose one bull for yourselves and prepare it first, for you are many; and call on the name of your god but put no fire under it.' So they took the bull which was given them, and they prepared it, and called on the name of Baal from morning till noon, saying, 'O Baal, hear us!' But there was no voice; no one answered. Then they leaped about the altar which they had made. And so it was, at noon, that Elijah mocked them and said, 'Cry aloud, for he is a god; either he is meditating, or he is busy, or he is on a journey, or perhaps he is sleeping and must be awakened.' So they cried aloud, and cut themselves, as was their custom, with knives and lances, until the blood gushed out on them. And when midday was past, they prophesied until the time of the offering of the evening sacrifice. But there was no voice, no one answered, no one paid attention. Then Elijah said to all the people, "Come near to me." So all the people came near to him. And he re-paired the altar of the LORD that was broken down. And Elijah took twelve stones, according to the number of the tribes of the sons of Jacob, to whom the word of the LORD had come, saying, 'Israel shall be your name.' Then with the stones he built an altar in the name of the LORD, and he made a trench around the altar large enough to hold two seahs of seed. And he put the wood in order, cut the bull in pieces and laid it on the wood, and said, 'Fill four waterpots with water, and pour it on the burnt sacrifice and on the wood.' Then he said, 'Do it a second time,' and they did it a second time; and he said, 'Do it a third time,' and they did it a third time. So the water ran all around the altar; and he also filled the trench with water. And it came to pass at the time of the offering of the evening sacrifice that Elijah, the prophet, came near and said, 'LORD God of Abraham, Isaac, and Israel, let it be known this day that you are God in

Israel and I am Your servant, and that I have done all these things at Your word Hear me, O LORD, hear me, that this people may know that You are the LORD God, and that You have turned their hearts back to You again.'" (This is the end of Elijah's prayer.)

Then the fire of the LORD fell and consumed the burnt sacrifice, and the wood and the stones, and the dust, and it licked up the water that was in the trench. Now when all the people saw it, they fell on their faces, and they said 'The LORD, He is God! The LORD, He is God!' And Elijah said to them 'Seize the prophets of Baal! Do not let one of them escape!' So they seized them; and Elijah brought them down to the Brook Kishon and executed them there."

This was no ordinary fire that consumed the entire sacrifice and all surrounding areas. It manifested itself to look like fire as the people knew it; however, it did more as it was a cleansing fire from heaven, God's fire, that is hotter than any other. He sent it to purify the souls of His people, to cleanse them with holy fire that saved the nation from pagan worship. Baal worship was an abomination to God Almighty.

This miracle was brought about through Elijah's devotion to God—his deep well with His Father through years of prayer and preparation for this time, and his brave boldness to do what God had called him. Elijah was duty driven to accomplish the will of God in his life. He came from the desert to the palace of the king. No one in their right mind would do such a thing, however, the anointing of God was upon Elijah, and he went with the surety that God had called him to this hour. Elijah knew that with God all things are possible!

He is a living testimony of faith and the power of prayer.

The drought ended

In 1King1 18:42-46 we read:

Then Elijah said to Ahab, 'Go up, eat and drink; for there is the sound of abundance of rain.' So Ahab went up to eat and drink. And Elijah went up to the top of Carmel; then he bowed down on the ground and put his face between his knees, and said to his servant, 'Go up now look toward the sea.' So he went up and looked, and said, 'There is nothing.' And seven times he said, 'Go again.' Then it came to pass the seventh time, that he said, 'There is a cloud, as small as a man's hand, rising out of the sea!' So he said, 'Go up and say to Ahab, 'Prepare your chariot, and go down before the rain stops you.' Now it happened in the meantime that the sky became black with clouds and wind, and there was a heavy rain. So Ahab rode away and went to Jezreel. The hand of the LORD came upon Elijah; and he girded up his loins and ran ahead of Ahab to the entrance of Jezreel.

We see in the small cloud—a cloud that is small as a man's hand—the great hand of God for with God little is much. With this small cloud came the end of a great drought upon the land through black clouds, wind and heavy rain. That is the difference in the size and power of man's hand and God Almighty's hand. The hand of God reaches to the *uttermost and accomplishes the miraculous.*

Elijah also exhibits the character trait of perseverance in prayer. He bowed down on the ground, put his face between his knees in reverence to God and prayed. Ahab, in contrast, went to eat and drink. Their celebration was completely different as Elijah went up to the top of Mount Carmel and prayed as he bowed down to the ground and put his head between his knees. He knew from whence his source of power came and he sought the face of God.

Ahab fed his physical body and Elijah his spiritual soul. In this very act, Elijah showed us the power of prayer. God used him through his journey on earth to be the vessel of many miracles; however, the true and remaining message was the *power of prayer.* For without this dimension in his life, *none* of these miracles would have flowed through him. Let us seek the throne of God with faith expecting to see the face of God and experience His miraculous love and grace extended to His people. *His* love story for us never ends.

Elijah escaped from Jezebel

1 Kings 19:1-10

And Ahab told Jezebel all that Elijah had done, also how he had executed all the prophets with a sword. Jezebel sent a messenger to Elijah, saying, 'So let the gods do to me, and more also, if I do not make your life as the life of one of them by tomorrow about this time.' And when he saw that, he arose and ran for his life, and went to Beersheba, which belongs to Judah, and left his servant there. But he himself went a day's journey into the wilderness and came and sat down under a broom tree. And he prayed that he might die, and said, 'It is enough! Now LORD take my life, for I am no better than my fathers!' Then as he lay and slept under a broom tree, suddenly an angel touched him, and said to him, 'Arise and eat.' Then he looked, and there by his head was a cake baked on coals, and a jar of water. So he ate and drank and lay down again. And the angel of the LORD came back the second time, and touched him, and said, 'Arise and eat, because the journey is too great for you.' So he arose and ate and drank; and he went in the strength of that food forty days and forty nights as far as Horeb, the mountain of God. And there he went into a cave, and spent the night in that place; and behold, the word of the LORD came to him, and said to him, *"What are you doing here, Elijah?"* So he said, "I have been very zealous for the LORD God of hosts; for the children of Israel have forsaken Your covenant, torn down Your altars, and killed Your prophets with a sword. I alone am left; and they seek to take my life."

After this great victory, we see Elijah cast down a bit, and he hastened a day's journey into the wilderness. He needed to be alone with God. When we stand strong against the enemy of our soul, we too need rest. He rested under a broom tree and prayed that he would die. He felt unworthy as he told his Father, "I am no better than my fathers." Elijah was weary and went to sleep under the broom. tree. Suddenly an angel appeared and urged him to get up and eat as he was tired from his journey. He saw a cake baked on coals, and a jar of water; food from heaven sent by an angel of God to feed this weary prophet. God was so good to provide nourishment and communion with a messenger from Him. Elijah went back to sleep and the angel came again, touched him, and said "Arise and eat, as the journey is too great for you." He stood up and he went in the strength of that food for forty days and forty nights far as Horeb, the mount of God." *(Elijah fasted forty days and forty nights.)* This was a great miracle. Heavenly food not only met his physical needs, but it also replenished his spiritual man. He was energized for the long trip to the Mount. There he entered a cave, once again away from all distractions and spent the night. The next day God spoke to him saying "What are you doing, Elijah?"

I see that he felt all alone when he told his Father In the words of 1 Kings 19:10: "So he said, "I have been very zealous for the LORD of hosts; for the children of Israel have forsaken Your covenant, torn down your altars, and killed Your prophets with the sword. I alone am left; and they seek to take my life."

We see the real root of his problem: he had done his best and now his enemies wanted to kill him. He felt abandoned. When we are tired, we do not see things as they really are because we are viewing them through the lens of our waning strength. Things always look worse than they are. Elijah was sad, alone, afraid, and needed to hear his Father's voice. What a comfort it is when we are depressed or cast down, and we hear God speaking to us. We then know that we can carry on and things are not as they seem. When we rest and commune with God, we see life in our spiritual reality, and it is positive. Our entire spirit changes and we know that we are more than able for the situation. Elijah needed encouragement. God provided that.

I do not think Elijah was clinically depressed. He had just experienced a miraculous victory against the Devil's religion. He was in spiritual warfare; the fire fell from heaven and the people cried out in Kings 18:39 *"The LORD, He is God! The LORD, He is God!"* Elijah instructed his followers to "Seize the prophets of Baal! Do not let one of them escape!" They seized them and Elijah brought them to the Brook Kishon and executed them. This was not an easy task as there were eight hundred-and-fifty of them and it took strength, dedication, and perseverance to accomplish this act. Now we know why Elijah needed to rest. His life was threatened by Jezebel, and this added an element of haste. Elijah was a strong man.

God's Revelation to Elijah

1 Kings 19:11-18:

Then He said, "Go out and stand on the mountain before the LORD." And behold, the LORD passed by, and a great and strong wind tore into the mountains and broke the rocks in pieces before the LORD, but the LORD was not in the wind; and after the wind an earthquake, but the LORD was not in the earthquake; and after the earthquake a fire, but the LORD was not in the fire; and after the fire a still small voice. So it was, when Elijah heard it, that he wrapped his face in his mantle and went out and stood in the entrance of the cave. Suddenly a voice came to him, and said, *"What are you doing here, Elijah?"* And he said, "I have been very zealous for the LORD God of hosts; because the children of Israel have forsaken Your covenant, torn down Your altars, and killed Your prophets with the sword. I alone am left, and they seek to take my life?" Then the LORD said to him: "'Go, return on your way to the Wilderness of Damascus, and when you arrive anoint Hazael as king over Syria. Also you shall anoint Jehu the son of Nimshi as king over Israel. And Elisha the son of Shaphat of Abel Meholah you shall anoint as prophet in your place. It shall be whoever escapes the sword of Hazael, Jehu will kill and whoever escapes the sword of Jehu, Elisha will kill. Yet I have reserved seven thousand in Israel, all whose knees have not bowed to Baal, and every mouth that has not kissed him."

The LORD had more work for Elijah to do. "God told him 'Go out and stand on the mountain before the LORD.'"

In this passage of scripture we see that the LORD passed by with a show of force and grandeur displayed in the mighty wind, the earthquake, and fire. The wind for purging, the earthquake for shaking and the fire for burning and cleansing. After the fire God came in a still, small voice, whereupon Elijah wrapped his face in his mantle out of reverence for God and he shielded his eyes from the great light, the Shekinah Glory of God—a blinding white light. A pure light that shines around God wherever He goes, for He truly is the "Light of the World." God then gave him specific instructions to go back to the wilderness of Damascus and anoint Hazael as King of Syria, anoint Jehu King of Israel, and to anoint Elisha as prophet in your place.

Elisha Followed Elijah

I Kings 19:19-21:

So he departed from there and found Elisha, the son of Shaphat, who was plowing with twelve yoke of oxen before him, and he was with the twelfth. Then Elijah passed by and threw his mantle on him. And he left the oxen and ran after Elijah, and said, 'Please let me kiss my father and my mother, and then I will follow you.' And he said to him, 'Go back again, for what have I done to you?' So Elisha turned back from him and took a yoke of oxen and slaughtered them and boiled their flesh, using the oxen's equipment, and gave it to the people, and they ate. Then he arose and followed Elijah and became his servant."

Elijah, in his abrupt manner, passed by and threw his mantle on Elisha. Elisha ran after him asking for permission to go back to his parents and say goodbye. He was granted that permission and the family gave him a "going away party." Elijah stayed for the party, and they left together with Elisha following God with his whole heart to serve the God of Israel in the office of prophet.

Elijah and Elisha were so closely connected to God that they were sure of their callings.

Elijah, King Ahaziah, and Fifty Captains

This story is found in 2 Kings Chapter One.

The book of 2 Kings continues the story that was begun in 1 Kings. Originally, the entire story was contained in only one scroll. Now let us begin this final journey of Elijah.

This story was written in 2 Kings 1:2-17. There was a conflict between those who worshiped Baal and those who worshiped the God of Israel. We know how zealous Elijah was for his God and that he was a great defender of Him. This was a battle fought in the physical realm with King Ahaziah, and in the spiritual realm, it was a war against the God of Israel.

King Ahab died and his son Ahaziah became king over Israel in Samaria. He ruled for only two years. He became an ungodly ruler who followed in the the tradition of his evil father. Ahaziah was a very loyal follower of Baal. He worshipped at the pagan shrines and that made the LORD God of Israel very angry. Ahaziah was as evil as his pagan father.

Ahaziah, this ardent worshipper, fell through the balcony railing in the upper room of his palace. He was severely injured. So much so that he sent for his messengers and told them, "Go, inquire of Baal-Zebub, the god of Ekron, whether I shall recover from this injury"(2 Kings 1:2).

God had heard all about this incident and sent an angel to Elijah the Tishbite, to instruct these messengers of Ahaziah saying, "Get up and go to the messengers of the king saying to them 'Is it because there is no God in Israel that you are going to inquire of Baal-Zebub, the god of Ekron'" 2 Kings 1:3)? And in 2 Kings 1:4 we read, "Now therefore, thus says the LORD: 'You shall not come down from the bed to which you have gone up, but you shall surely die.'" So Elijah departed.

When the messengers returned immediately the king was upset and asked them why they came back so soon. They told him about a man they had met. The man told them to return to the king and say to him, "Thus says the Lord: 'Is it because there is no God in Israel that you are going to ask Baal-Zebub the god of Ekron? Therefore you shall not come down from the bed to which you have gone up, but you shall surely die'"(2 Kings 1:6).

The king immediately wanted to know more about this man. The messengers told him that he was a hairy man who wore a leather belt about his waist. King Ahaziah immediately said, "It is Elijah the Tishbite" (2 Kings 1:8).

Now the captains get involved with this situation. The king sent a captain with fifty men to find Elijah. They found him sitting on top of a hill. And the captain said, "Man of God, the king has said 'Come down'" (1Kings 1:9). Elijah answered and said to the captain of fifty "If that is true let fire come down from heaven and consume you and your fifty men."

And fire did come down from heaven and consumed him and his fifty (2 Kings 1:10).

This did not faze the evil King so he sent another captain with fifty men. This captain said to Elijah, "Man of God, the king said,'Come down quickly'" (2 Kings 1:11)! Elijah had the same response, "If I am a man of God, let fire come down from heaven and consume you and your fifty men." And the fire of God came down and killed the him and his fifty (2 Kings 1:12).

The king sent another captain with fifty men. This third captain went to Elijah and "fell on his knees and pleaded with him saying, 'Man of God, please let my life and the life of my servants of yours be precious in your sight. Look, fire has come down from heaven and burned up the first two captains of fifties with their fifties. Please let my life be precious in your sight'" (2 Kings 1:13-14). The angel of the LORD spoke to Elijah saying, "Go down with him; do not be afraid of him" (2 Kings 1:15). Elijah heeded the words of the angel and went down with him to the king. In 2 Kings 1:16 Elijah said to King Ahaziah, "Thus says the LORD: 'Because you have sent messengers to enquire of Baal-Zebub, the god of Ekron, is it because there is no God in Israel to inquire of His word? Therefore you shall not come down from the bed to which you have gone up, but you shall surely die.'"

And Ahaziah died according to the message of the LORD that was delivered through the prophet Elijah. God sent down fire to devour these evil men. Elijah's actions were defensive and an act of God's judgment on idolatry. He walked so closely with God that he could hear his voice and follow His instructions. This was a fierce battle between the Devil's army and God's army. Elijah, once again, was the defender of the faith as he stood strong for the God of Israel. God had put His trust in Elijah.

The fiercer the battle the greater the reward.

Elijah is translated

And it came to pass, when the LORD was about to take up Elijah into heaven by a whirlwind, that Elijah went with Elisha from Gilgal. Then Elijah said to Elisha, 'Stay here, please, for the LORD has sent me on to Bethel.' But Elisha said, 'As the LORD lives, and as your soul lives, I will not leave you!' So they went down to Bethel. Now the sons of the prophets who were at Bethel came out to Elisha, and said to him, 'Do you know that the LORD will take away your master from over you today?' And he said, 'Yes, I know; keep silent!' Then Elijah said to him, 'Elisha, stay here, please, for the LORD has sent me on to Jericho.' But he said, 'As the LORD lives, and as your soul lives, I will not leave you!' So they came to Jericho. Now the sons of the prophets who were at Jericho came to Elisha and said to him, 'Do you know that the LORD will take away your master from over you today?' So he answered, 'Yes, I know; keep silent!' Then Elijah said to him, 'Stay here, please, for the LORD has sent me on to the Jordan.' But he said, 'As the LORD lives and as your soul lives, I will not leave you!' So the two of them went on. And fifty men of the sons of the prophets went and stood facing them at a distance, while the two of them stood by the Jordan. Now Elijah took his mantle, rolled it up, and struck the water; and it was divided this way and that, so that the two of them crossed over on dry ground. And so it was, when they had crossed over, that Elijah said to Elisha, 'Ask! What may I do for you, before I am taken away from you?' Elisha said, 'Please let a double portion of your spirit be upon me.' So he said, 'You have asked a hard thing. Nevertheless, if you see me when I am taken from you, it shall be so for you; but if not, it shall not be so.' Then it happened as they continued on and talked, that suddenly, a chariot of fire appeared with horses of fire, and separated the two of them; and Elijah went up by a whirlwind into heaven. And Elisha saw it, and he cried out, 'My father, my father, the chariot of Israel and its horsemen!' So he saw him no more. And he took hold of his own clothes and tore them into two pieces. Then had he also took up the mantle of Elijah that had fallen from him and went back and stood by the bank of the Jordan. Then he took the mantle of Elijah that had fallen from him, and struck the water, and said, 'Where is the LORD God of Elijah?' And when he also had struck the water, it was divided this way and that; and Elisha crossed over. Now when the sons of the prophets who were from Jericho saw him, they said, 'The spirit of Elijah rests on Elisha.' And they came to meet him and bowed to the ground before him. Then they said to him, 'Look now, there are fifty strong men with your servants, Please let them go and search for your master, lest perhaps the Spirit of the LORD has taken him up and cast him upon some mountain or into some valley.' And he said, 'You shall not send anyone.'

And when they had urged him until he was ashamed, he said, 'Send them!' Therefore they sent fifty men, and they searched for three days but did not find him. And when they came back to him, for he had stayed in Jericho, he said to them, 'Did I not say to you, 'Do not go''' (2 Kings: 2:1-18)?

This passage contains scripture that relates the events just prior to Elijah leaving this earth as abruptly as he arrived as well as his a grand departure. God had designed a special chariot with special horses to take His beloved prophet back to Himself. He ferried him to heaven in a special whirlwind that represented the Spirit of God. He left no doubt that He was pleased with the service Elijah had accomplished through His power on earth, and rewarded him with an unforgettable, miraculous exit from earth. Elijah was a great man of prayer and faith. He is often called the Confrontational Prophet because of the holy boldness that he possessed. To God be the Glory!

CHAPTER 9
Elijah: In Review

Elijah's name means "God is Jehovah." He was given a name that would reflect what he would become in the kingdom of God on earth, or a reminder of the might and holiness of God. Elijah was born in Tisbe, a village among the mountains of Gilead, east of the Jordan River. Little is known about his childhood. He was reared by a Jewish family, his father was Sadock, and his mother was unknown. God chose Elijah long before his birth because He knew that Elijah would be a strong man who sought Him, and He would teach him the power of prayer. As a young child, Elijah prayed to God and began to develop his faith. By the time he reached manhood he was ready for the ministry that God had prepared for him.

His village was often attacked by Nomadic tribes, and this taught him to be brave and bold, to stand against adversity expecting to overcome it. This background prepared him for his fight against paganism. A brave prayer warrior he was! He probably had no education or schooling; however, he was spiritually instructed by God, His Father, who had a great journey prepared for him.

It is interesting that history reveals that Elijah was a beloved prophet and recorded as one of the greatest prophets in Bible history. There have been many artists that have painted him. Art history reveals that in 1565 AD Paolo Farinati drew "Elijah and the Chariot of Fire" on white paper measuring sixteen-by-twelve-inches. The drawing was done with with pen and ink and wash over black chalk. Farinai had been commissioned to paint a large fresco. This a drawing he did in preparation to complete this work of art.

Sir Godfrey Kneller painted "Elijah and the Angel" in 1672 AD. Kneller was born in Germany and settled permanently in England. This painting depicts Elijah's flight into the wilderness to escape the evil Queen Jezebel. He fell asleep and was awakened by an angel who gave him bread and water. God showed how much He loved and appreciated what Elijah was doing. This work of art was oil paint on canvas and measured six-by-five feet. The artist became the leading portrait painter of his day. He valued this piece of art so much that he brought it to his home in Whitton, Middlesex.

Johann Friedrich Overbeck, a German artist, drew "The Prophet Elijah Casting his Mantle over Elisha," in 1835 AD. This rendition was done in black lithographic chalk on off-white paper and measured ten-by-twelve-inches.

These paintings of Elijah were done many years ago showing how Elijah was revered. They honored his work for his LORD.

Elijah was also honored by the Roman Catholic Church and is celebrated each year on July 20. Members of the Carmelite

Order took him as their patron saint during their transition from the slopes of Mt. Carmel in Palestine to urban life in medieval Europe. This order was established in the twelfth century revealing that the early church acknowledged Elijah's work and the fact that he was chosen by God.2

The Greek Orthodox Church also honors Elijah on July 20. They celebrate his life and his great devotion to God. This great devotion established a phenomenal relationship with His Father which brought many miracles in his life and ministry.

God Miraculously Met Elijah at Every Event in His Life.

He had fed him with divine food:

1 Kings 17:6: "The ravens brought him bread and meat in the morning, and bread and meat in the evening; and he drank from the brook."

1 Kings 17:14-15: "For thus says the LORD God of Israel: 'The bin of flour shall not be used up, nor the jar of oil run dry, until the day the LORD sends rain on the earth.' So she went away and did according to the word of Elijah; and she and he and her household ate for many days.

1 Kings 19:5-8: "Then as he lay and slept under a juniper tree, suddenly an angel touched him and said to him, 'Arise and eat.' Then he looked and there by his head was a cake baked on coals, and a jar of water. So he ate and drank and lay down again. And the angel of the Lord came back the second time, and touched him, and said, 'Arise and eat, because the

journey is too great for you.' So he arose and ate and drank; and he went in the strength of that food forty days and forty nights as far as Horeb, the mountain of God."

He was a fearless reformer:

1 Kings 18:40: This reveals Elijah's great Mount Carmel victory against the prophets of Baal. He called down fire from heaven destroying the altar and the area surrounding the altar. It is written in 1 Kings 18:40: "And Elijah said to them, 'Seize the prophets of Baal! Do not let one escape!' So they seized them; and Elijah brought them down to the Brook Kishon and executed them there."

He rebuked kings:

1 Kings 21:20: "So Ahab said to Elijah, 'Have you found me, O my enemy?' And he answered, 'I have found you, because you have sold yourself to do evil in the sight of the LORD.'"

2 Kings 1:16: "Then he (Elijah) said to him (King Ahaziah), "Thus says the LORD: 'Because you have sent messengers to inquire of Baal-Zebub, the god of Ekron, is it because there is no God in Israel to inquire of His word? Therefore you shall not come down from the bed to which you have gone up, but you shall surely die'"

He was a mighty prayer warrior:

1 Kings 17:20-22:

"Then he cried out to the LORD and said, 'O LORD my God, have You also brought tragedy to the widow with whom I lodge, by killing her son?' And he stretched himself out on the child three times, and cried out to the LORD and said, 'O LORD my God, I pray, let this child's soul come back to him.' Then the LORD heard the voice of Elijah; and the soul of the child came back to him, and he revived."

1 Kings 18:36-38:

"And it came to pass, at the time of the offering of the evening sacrifice, that Elijah the prophet came near and said, 'LORD God of Abraham, Isaac, and Israel, let it be known this day that You are God in Israel and I am Your servant, and that I have done all these things at Your word. Hear me, O LORD, hear me, that this people may know that You are the LORD God, and that You have turned their hearts back to You again.' Then the fire of the LORD fell and consumed the burnt sacrifice, and the wood and the stones and the dust, and it licked up the water that was in the trench."

James 5:17-18: "Elijah was a man with a nature like ours, and he prayed earnestly that it would not rain; and it did not rain on the land for three years and six months. And he prayed again, and the heaven gave rain, and the earth produced its fruit."

He became tired and discouraged:

1 Kings 19:3-4: "And when he saw that, he arose and ran for his life, and went to Beersheba, which belongs to Judah, and left his servant there. But he himself went a day's journey into the wilderness and came and sat down under a broom tree. And he prayed that he might die, and said, 'It is enough! Now, LORD, take my life, for I am no better than my fathers!'" Prior to this scripture passage, Jezebel had threatened to take his life and he fled.

God honored Elijah:

2 Kings 2:11: "**Then it happened,** as they continued on and talked, that suddenly a chariot of fire appeared with horses of fire and separated the two of them, and Elijah went up by a whirlwind into heaven." What an honor! God wanted Elijah with Him, and He took him!

Matt. 17:3: "And behold, Moses and Elijah appeared to them, talking with Him." Another honor is bestowed on Elijah. This was the gathering with Jesus, Peter, James and John on the Mount of Transfiguration.

Elijah wrote four verses in the Old Testament:

Elijah was not a writing prophet; however, he wrote four verses in the Bible prophesying the sickness and death of an evil king. King Jehoram had rejected the righteous way of his father, King Jehosophat, as well as those of King Asa who was also king of Judah. This is an interesting fact because Elijah was probably translated before or during the reign of Jehoshaphat. Elijah may have given the letter to a trusted servant to deliver it to Jehoram at the appropriate time.

This story is recorded in 2 Chronicles 21:12-15:

"And a letter came to King Jehoram from Elijah the prophet saying, 'Thus says the LORD God of your Father David: Because you have not walked in the ways of Jehoshaphat your father, or in the ways of Asa king of Judah, but have walked in the way of the kings of Israel, and have made Judah and the inhabitants of Jerusalem to play the harlot like the harlotry of the house of Ahab, and also have killed your brothers, those of your father's household, who *were better* than yourself, behold, the LORD will strike your people with a serious affliction—your children, your wives, and all your possessions; and you *will become* very sick with a disease of your intestines, until your intestines come out by reason of the sickness, day by day."

After this the LORD struck Jehoram with an incurable disease of the intestines. He suffered with this disease for two years. He died in severe pain. In 2 Chronicles: 21:20 we read, "He was thirty-two years old when he became king. He reigned in Jerusalem eight years and, to no one's sorrow, departed. However, they buried him in the City of David, but not in the tombs of the kings."

His legacy as a king was one of a pagan reign, and he died without honor.

In this case Elijah was like the trumpet of God announcing a penalty for sickness and, as such, standing tall for the holiness of God as he had all his life.

CHAPTER 10
Songs of Praise

The Song of the Bow: David's Song for Jonathan and Saul

We find the following passage in 2 Samuel 1:19-27:

> "The beauty of Israel is slain on your high places!
> How the mighty have fallen!
> Tell it not in Gath,
> Proclaim it not in the streets of Ashkelon—
> Lest the daughters of the Philistines rejoice,
> Lest the daughters of the uncircumcised triumph.
>
> "O mountains of Gilboa,
> Let there be no dew nor rain upon you,
> Nor fields of offerings.
> For the shield of the mighty is cast away there!
> The shield of Saul, not anointed with oil.
> From the blood of the slain,
> From the fat of the mighty,
> The bow of Jonathan did not turn back,
> And the sword of Saul did not return empty.

"Saul and Jonathan were beloved and pleasant in their lives,
And in their death they were not divided;
They were swifter than eagles,
They were stronger than lions.

"O daughters of Israel, weep over Saul,
Who clothed you in scarlet, with luxury;
Who put ornaments of gold on your apparel.

"How the mighty have fallen in the midst of the battle!
Jonathan was slain in your high places.
I am distressed for you, my brother Jonathan;
You have been very pleasant to me;
Your love to me was wonderful,
Surpassing the love of women.

"How the mighty have fallen,
And the weapons of war perished!"

The title of this song was very important as the bow and arrow were symbols of military might. The tribe of Benjamin was known for their great military power and their skill with the bow and arrow. The words "How the mighty have fallen," were recorded in two verses of the song. David is speaking of Jonathan and Saul and honoring them for their bravery in battle.

David encouraged the people of Judah to teach their children this song. David was a gifted musician, a great warrior, and an anointed King. He was a "man after God's own heart" (Acts 13:22).

Hannah's Song of Prayer

We find the following passage in 1 Samuel 2:1-10:

"My heart rejoices in the LORD;
My horn is exalted in the LORD,
I smile at my enemies,
Because I rejoice in Your salvation.

"No one is holy like the LORD,
For there is none besides You,
Nor is there any rock like our God.

"Talk no more so very proudly;
Let no arrogance come from your mouth,
For the LORD is the God of knowledge;
And by Him actions are weighed.

"The bows of the mighty men are broken,
And those who stumbled are girded with strength.
Those who were full have hired themselves out for bread,
And the hungry have ceased *to hunger.*
Even the barren has borne seven,
And she who has many children has become feeble.

"The LORD kills and makes alive;
He brings down to the grave and brings up.

The LORD makes poor and makes rich;
He brings low and lifts up.
He raises the poor from the dust
And lifts the beggar from the ash heap,
To set them among princes
And make them inherit the throne of glory.

"For the pillars of the earth are the LORD's,
And He has set the world upon them.
He will guard the feet of His saints,
But the wicked shall be silent in darkness.

"For by strength no man shall prevail
The adversaries of the LORD shall be broken in pieces;
From heaven He will thunder against them.
The LORD will judge the ends of the earth.

"He will give strength to His king,
And exalt the horn of His anointed."

Hannah wrote this song after she had weaned Samuel and brought him to Eli. She reminded Eli that she was the woman who prayed for this child and God had answered her prayers. In 1 Sam 1:28 we we find Hannah saying: "Therefore, I also have lent him to the LORD; as long as he lives he shall be lent to the LORD." So they worshiped the LORD there.

CONCLUSION

Through the course of this book I've attempted to crystallize for the reader the spiritual disciplines that have proven very powerful in my life, bringing me into an intimacy with God that would not have otherwise been possible.

First, we saw how the act of fasting revolutionized the lives of the heroes in scripture. From Hannah, who desperately longed for a child, to King David, who, was pursued by determined enemies and sought God's protection and guidance to Jehoshaphat, who proclaimed a fast for the entire nation of Judah for deliverance from mighty enemy troops. We witnessed, through scripture, the steadfast efficacy of prayer and fasting. This proves beyond a doubt that those two weapons in our spiritual arsenal must not be neglected. May we never forget that pivotal moment in history when Jehoshaphat admitted that he and his countrymen did not know what to do, but their eyes were on God for deliverance, for comfort and for direction! How often do we find ourselves in this situation? May we never forget what prayer accomplished for Jehoshaphat! His enemies were thrown into confusion and failed against him!

We also witnessed the repentance of the wicked city of Nineveh as evidenced and ushered in by the act of fasting and how the lifestyle of prayer practiced by Nehemiah resulted in rebuilding of the wall around the holy city of Jerusalem. We saw Nehemiah confronted time and again by enemies sent to distract and detract from the rebuilding of the wall, and yet, as Nehemiah took each challenge to God in prayer, success marked his endeavors. He reminded the people that God would fight for them. As a result, the holy city was repopulated, and the proper worship of God was re-established there.

I pray you were encouraged to fast and pray in your individual lives as we walked through the challenges of Queen Esther who fasted, prayed, and exhorted the Jews in her city of Shushan to do likewise. The lives of all her people *were spared* from a diabolical plot as a result of her faithfulness. Likewise the prophetess Anna, who had devoted her life to prayer and fasting was given the gift of seeing her Savior face-to-face. We learned of Cornelius, the gentile whose entire household came to faith in Christ as a result of a revelation that came to him as he fasted. The apostle Paul was sent to preach the good news. Cornelius' close relationship with God and his acts of prayer and fasting opened the way. Paul himself, we learned, fasted before his conversion. He went on to become one of the greatest heroes of the faith known to mankind.

Let us not forget Daniel, who was faithful in prayer and received great revelations as a result. His mind was enlightened to many truths of the future, including the rebuilding of Jerusalem, the holy city.

We also saw that Jesus Christ, our greatest example, fasted forty days before He was tempted in the wilderness. This scene set the stage for our success in spiritual warfare by the power of the Holy Spirit for the ages to come!

I have attempted, throughout the course of this book, to stress the importance of a heart that is "set on pilgrimage" (Psalm 84:5). I hope the reader was able to discern that finding intimacy with God is a very intentional act, which is why we journeyed through the lives of people like the prophet Enoch who sought the LORD with his whole heart and was not disappointed. We saw that he did not taste earthly death, but was rather taken up into heaven to be with God who cherished him. We saw Simeon and Anna, two who devoted themselves to seeking God and were rewarded with a few moments in the physical presence of Jesus after a lifetime of looking toward His coming.

It is my express desire that the reader come away with a sense that, while intimacy with God is available to every believer, it is borne of a process that involves daily intentionality. While it is true that the Holy Spirit will absolutely do the heavy lifting in the process of sanctification, we must make ourselves available. We must sit and marinate in His presence as I imagine King Solomon did. The results were the treasure trove of wisdom found in the Proverbs.

I spent a great deal of time on Elijah because his life represents the ultimate exchange: a laying down of self and a receipt of unparalleled devine power, closeness with God, and a heavy anointing of the Holy Spirit. We saw, that in exchange for his very life, Elijah was allowed to return God's people to Himself. He put the prophets of Baal to shame in the display of divine power unforeseen and never replicated. Finally, this man of God who sought his Father with abandon and was taken up into heaven in a chariot of fire pulled by horses of fire. Elijah was a man like any other man. The difference was that he recognized his calling and he pressed into it with all the life he had been given.

The message for the rest of us? When we meet with the LORD daily, making ourselves available through prayer and the reading of His word, He comes to meet with us. We *WILL* experience ever-increasing levels of intimacy with God as we practice the disciplines of prayer, fasting and waiting on God. It is also important to take time to record what He says to us. We will be on an adventure like no other with the only almighty God of the Universe.

NOTES

Hastings, John, ed. *The Great Men and Women of the Bible,* Vol. 1. New York: Charles Scribner's Sons, 1949

Torrey, R.A. *Topical Textbook,* Murfreesboro, Tennessee: Sword of the Lord, 2000.

[1] Baden, Joel. "God Opened Her Womb--- The Biblical Conception of Fertility." The Torah accessed 12 June 2021, https://www.thetorah.com/article/god-opened-her-womb-the-biblical-conception-of-fertility.

McClintock, John, and James Strong. *Cyclopedia of Biblical, Theological and Ecclesiastical Literature*: *12 Volumes.* Grand Rapids, Michigan: Baker Book House, 1969.

[2] "Privacy Policy," Privacy & Terms, Google, last modified April 17, 2017, https://www.google.com/policies/privacy/.

Kristi Woods," Who Was Elijah and Why Is His Bible Study Still Important Today? 20 July 2018, (https:www.crosswalk.com/faith/bible-study/who-was-Elijah.html).